JESSE

LIFE

RESURRECTED

Extraordinary Miracles Through Ordinary People

KUDU

"Verily, verily, I say unto you, The hour is coming, and now is, when the dead shall hear the voice of the Son of God: and they that hear shall live. For as the Father hath life in himself; so hath he given to the Son to have life in himself; And hath given him authority to execute judgment also, because he is the Son of man. Marvel not at this: for the hour is coming, in the which all that are in the graves shall hear his voice, And shall come forth; they that have done good, unto the resurrection of life; and they that have done evil, unto the resurrection of damnation."

— John 5:25-29

Life Resurrected:
Extraordinary Miracles Through Ordinary People

by Jesse Birkey
copyright ©2012 by Jesse Birkey

Trade paperback ISBN: 9781938624193
Ebook ISBN: 9781938624209

Cover design by Jeff Damm

Life Resurrected is also available on Amazon Kindle, Barnes &
Noble Nook and Apple iBooks.

Published by Kudu Publishing (*kudupub.com*) in conjunction
with Light Force Publishing (*operationlightforce.com*).

CONTENTS

ACKNOWLEDGEMENTS

I want to thank my wife, Kara, for traveling this road of discovery with me. It hasn't always been an easy road and you have been there to help me find the middle when I wanted to set up camp on an extreme side. Thank you for being the voice of balance, correction, love, support and encouragement. God has repeatedly shown me that I need you by my side.

Thanks to Richard Mull and Light Force Publishing for taking on this project. You have seen the passion of my heart and shared in it. These last years would look completely different if you weren't a part of them and I am so grateful to have you in my life.

Thanks to Kudu Publishing for partnering with us in this project. Your experience and wisdom are priceless. Every time I meet with your team I am touched by the sincerity of your hearts that have been shaped by God. Thanks for believing in this project.

Thanks to all of you "ordinary people" who have contributed to this project. This book wouldn't be the same without your stories. God has used many people to make this book special. Your stories are going to touch and inspire many lives.

With deep appreciation,

Jesse Birkey

ENDORSEMENTS

Recently I heard a very close relative tell me that their heart was passionate for a closer relationship with Father God but every time they got into some sort of discipline it seemed so stale. They wanted more but did not know what to do. To suggest any advice at that moment did not seem the appropriate thing to do. I also had not at that time read this book. In Jesse Birkey's book *Life Resurrected* he provokes us to do something with our stale relationship with Father God. This book is really a testimony of not just Jesse's life change but of so many people in crisis that Father allows Jesse the privilege of being a part of their life change. He encounters these people in the most unusual ways, generally a life crisis, and Father pours through Jesse the power of Love that actually does everything from change a situation to literally raising people from the dead and giving them a second chance. So many of us need another chance at life to encounter a powerful, passionate relationship that will not be stale. I loved reading the testimonies of how when Jesse prayed for the people he came in contact with during the day that Father answered those prayers. Simple huh? It should be, but for so many of us this is not our experience. This book rekindles the passion to be passionate with Him. I highly recommend it for anyone who wants to facilitate the Love and Power of the Bible through their relationship with a loving, kind God.

— *Trisha Frost*
An ordinary follower of Jesus
Shiloh Place Ministries

When I started to read this book I did not expect how deeply each chapter would impact me. God spoke to me through the chapters and confirmed that I am truly hearing His voice. My confidence as well as my boldness to approach people with a word or encouragement from the Lord grew with every testimony I read. I found encouragement to keep on seeking the Lord and confirmation that our God is still in the miracle business. Jesse Birkey, a firefighter, finds a close relationship with the Lord. His calling is to show others who God is. *"Show them who I am. Help them understand My love by living in it. Bear My testimony to the people."*(p.156) His example shows that God uses ordinary people to bring healing and freedom. The only thing that we have to do is to draw closer to Him and to listen and obey God. I was tremendously impacted when Jesse shared about the time he asked the Lord to break his heart for what breaks His. *"It felt like the power of all the grief and unimaginable sadness was going to rip me apart."*(p.113) God showed Jesse how his sin affected Him. Wow! God has such a deep love for us; a love that is beyond our comprehension. It is a love that forgives, restores, heals, and lasts forever. This image of God will be with me for the rest of my life and help me stay on the narrow path set before me.

—*Silke Buczynsky*
An ordinary follower of Jesus

It was a privilege to read this book, and has helped my husband and I define some very tormenting things in our relationship that we were never able to quite define before. Thank you for your courage and transparency... it will surely result in eternal fruit! This book has blessed me!

—*Kelly Noto*
An ordinary follower of Jesus

FOREWORD

I have to say that I am so proud of Jesse. Not as much for writing his second book as for the man of God He has become, how he goes after God and follows hard after him. This is the biggest reason this book is what it is.

This book will grab readers as soon as they pick it up. The stories are real and true. I am fortunate to know almost everyone mentioned in his book. I've seen God's power at work in my own life, in and through Jesse's life and in the lives of other ordinary people.

Jesse dared to believe God's Word and that God was still alive and could do the same things today that He did through ordinary people like some fishermen, a tax collector and a doctor two thousand years ago. It changed his life, and God through Jesse has changed the lives of many people.

He's not a TV evangelist and may never have a megachurch or his name up in lights but he has seen more miracles, more dead raised and more men and women set free than most people that I know in ministry at megachurches.

I wonder, if Jesus were here today who He would hang out with? I believe it would be a group of ordinary guys like Jesse who would dare to believe, lay it all down and follow Him.

I honestly believe that this is one of the most compelling books you may ever read. It is not the story of one miracle but of daily miracles. It is not the story of an American idol, a sports superstar, or multi-millionaire financial success, or like any of the other books that garner so much attention. This book is about someone just like you! He had fears, insecurities, and major problems but it all looked fine on the outside. Then God began to transform him and show him what it meant for Jesus to be in him. He began to believe that God really lived in him and that this gave him power and authority. He began to listen to and follow God.

The result in Jesse's life from what He is sharing with you is that he regularly sees the sick healed, captives set free and even the dead raised. How would you like to experience a transformed life and see God healing people, setting them free and God doing extraordinary miracles through you?

— Richard Mull
President and founder of Operation Light Force
Best-selling author of *The 40-Day Revolution*
and *The Jesus Training Manual*

PREFACE

It was dark and stormy. The waves were beating against the small boat and the winds were strong. Who knew how much more the boat could take. It was three o'clock in the morning and the whole crew was awake, trying to maintain control of the vessel. Some on the boat had been in this position before. A few of them were fishermen and were sometimes more at home on the sea than on land. But that didn't mean any of them enjoyed a bad storm.

Anxiety levels and stress were high. Fear was beginning to set in and move through those with less experience on the sea. The fear was contagious and soon every member on board was feeling uneasy.

Suddenly, something was spotted coming toward the boat. It was hard to see but it seemed like something was floating across the water. They could only see it because it carried a soft glow. There were shouts of fright as it moved closer. It was coming right at them. As it steadily drew closer the men on board could see that it was a man. Now fear went to the next level. It was certainly a ghost. What else could it be? The closer it got the more defined the shape became. There were cries throughout the deck as men trembled, sure that this morning would be their last.

Then the being did what could only cause those on the edge of passing out to go all the way. It spoke! The words took all on board by surprise. The ghost man said with a voice carrying far above the sounds of rushing wind and crashing waves, "Take courage! I AM! Stop being afraid!"

The words thundered through the men's souls and lit their hearts on fire. The cries stopped as the revelation hit them in an instant. It wasn't a ghost. It was Jesus. It was Jesus and He was standing on the water about thirty feet from the boat.

For a moment nobody said a word. Then a man who had always been eager to prove himself stood and leaned over the boat. He shouted, "Lord, if it is you, command me to come to you on the

13

water." The man was called Peter and he wanted to be with his master. Jesus answered him with a voice soft yet somehow powerful enough to make the wind and waves seem like whispers, "Come."

Peter promptly lifted his legs over the side of the boat and lowered himself onto the water. The whole time he kept his eyes on Jesus. Jesus held His place with His hand extended as Peter walked toward the object of his love.

Then a wave crashed and Peter hesitated. The rest of the crew back on board held their collective breath. Peter froze, taking his eyes off of Jesus. He looked around and began to tremble. All he could see were the deadly waves. It was then that he began to sink. Terror gripped his heart. He frantically tried to lift his feet but it was useless. His solid foundation had gone. Aware that he couldn't help himself he cried out to Jesus in desperation. "Lord, save me!" No sooner were the words out of his mouth than Jesus ran to him and grasped Peter's arm. Jesus pulled him up and held him steady. Jesus' words were soft and loving but full of sorrow: "O you of little faith, why did you doubt?"

Jesus and Peter walked back to the boat together and climbed over the edge. As soon as Jesus was in the boat the wind stopped blowing and the sea calmed. Everyone on board was overcome and fell down in worship. A loud cry rose from the depths of their hearts, "Truly You are the Son of God!"

This is a story from Matthew 14:24-33. I chose to open with this story because it illustrates the purpose of this book so well. There was nothing extraordinary about the men gathered on the boat. They were from all different walks of life. They didn't have titles or ministries. I would venture to say that none of them had a household name. In fact, some of them weren't liked very much at all. Matthew was a tax collector. We know that tax collectors were very much despised. It's possible that none of them ever led a Bible study or led worship.

Yet here was Peter ready to perform the miraculous. He obviously never got the memo that ordinary people can't walk on water. In the pages ahead you will find powerful testimonies to encourage you, comfort you, inspire you, and give you hope to carry on. You will learn how God has used ordinary people in powerful ways. You will see that the command Jesus gave to Peter when He told him to "Come" wasn't just for Peter. Jesus has given us an open invitation to step into His life! It's an extraordinary life and the open invitation is birthed out of God's love for us; It's birthed out of God's love for **you**.

But Peter took his eyes off of Jesus. I have also taken my eyes off of Jesus as I have learned to walk with Him. In this book, you will learn how God set me free from a life of bondage and slavery to the enemy. It wasn't until I embraced heart transformation that God began to build testimonies in me. The greatest testimony I have is the work of transformation God did in me, changing almost everything about me. He took my cold heart and made it warm clay to be shaped and molded by His hands.

Peter was sinking and he cried out to the Lord in desperation. He realized that Jesus didn't change the structure of the water or change him in any way. It wasn't that Jesus made Peter's body lighter than the water. Peter realized that it was his faith and trust in Jesus that gave him the ability to survive in the raging sea. As soon as his faith was broken he began to sink. It was all about Jesus and His ability. He cried out and Jesus was right there by his side to save him.

Peter's experience represents most of us. He represents those who at first eagerly pursue Jesus in zeal, keeping their eyes on Him and seeing amazing things. He also represents those of us who take our eyes off of Him mid-journey, those of us who are stuck and feel like we are dying. He represents those who need forgiveness and those who need Jesus to just hold them for a while. What he represents is our journey of heart transformation in all of its stages.

My vision for this book is to give you a view of what the journey of heart transformation might look like and to provide insight into the ways God wants to operate in and through you. This book will alternate between my journey of transformation and powerful testimonies of ordinary people seeking to be used by God. I hope that as you read you will realize that the freedom I have experienced is available to you as well and that God wants to give you amazing testimonies.

Jesus said in Mark 16:17 that signs and wonders would *follow* those who *believe*. But that word *"believe"* is not to be taken lightly. It's so much more than a simple spoken confession (Rom. 10:9-10). God is intensely concerned with reconciling us to Himself (John 20:30-31; 2 Cor. 5:18-21), so we must also intensely desire intimate relationship with Him. We must not seek signs and wonders apart from intentionally surrendering our hearts to Him (Matt. 12:38-39; 1 Cor. 1:22-23). I began to pursue intimacy with Him *before* he started to use me in miraculous ways.

God doesn't require us to finish the journey of transformation before He'll work through us. He just wants us to begin. I believe that's the way He wants it for all of us. So let's start the race marked out for us (Heb. 12:1).

CHAPTER 1

FROM DEATH TO LIFE

"Miracles are a retelling in small letters of the very same story which is written across the whole world in letters too large for some of us to see." – C.S. Lewis

It was just about eleven o'clock one night at fire station number twelve where I was assigned. I was just about to get into bed, when the tones went off in the station, signaling an emergency. I straightened up and quickly got myself ready to respond.

As our crew of four piled into the fire engine and the rescue (ambulance), we heard dispatch tell us that this was a medical call and that the patient was unconscious. During the previous year, God had begun a life-changing work in me. He had made crystal clear my desperate need for Him. (I'll share that story a little later). Not only my need for Him in my life away from work, but at work as well. God revealed to me just how much I cared what others thought and how that obsession was crippling my testimony. How could I be obedient to Jesus when I cared more about what others thought than what He thought? How could I be obedient to Jesus when I was afraid that saying "yes" to Him might cost me my job? But the Lord had encountered me in a way I couldn't ignore and by His grace and His strength I decided to say "yes" to God, no matter what. I had counted the cost and had finally decided to be a willing vessel. But this "willing vessel" stuff was still pretty new to me. The fear of what might happen if it became known that I was praying for people in the back of the rescue was a tough thing to overcome and it had me on an emotional roller coaster. To go with that, what had I really ever seen in my life to give me the kind of faith to believe that God can heal the sick or raise the dead and why in the world would He want to use me in those ways? The answers to those questions were, "Not very much" and, "I have no idea." But that night, after many years of ignoring God while I was at work as a firefighter/paramedic, I was getting my first opportunity to step out in faith. With this in mind, along with some anxiety, I began to wonder what God might have me do.

We were just about on scene when the call was upgraded to a cardiac arrest. Those words have a way of raising the anxiety level for everyone responding. As we pulled up to the house, I began to pray quietly. For the first time ever I prayed against death and destruction and prayed that God would heal the stranger I was about to meet. I was trying to have faith, but I wasn't feeling very confident. It was like I was trying to draw from a well that was only a little wet at the bottom. I was more than a little irritated at God for dropping a cardiac arrest in my lap instead of something much easier to warm up with.

My partner and I entered the house and found a man lying on the floor next to his bed. The man did not respond to my voice or to anything we did to try to wake him. I felt for a pulse and found nothing. The man wasn't breathing and was cold and pale. He was dead. My heart sank, and hope lost ground. My prayers didn't seem to be working at all. I began to feel a little foolish and heard that horrible voice in my ear saying, *"See, God isn't with you. You're an idiot."* We worked as fast as we could to get the heart monitor set up and to get oxygen going. As we did, I suddenly felt some resolve course through me, and again I quietly prayed against death and asked God to heal the poor man. I wasn't sure if my partner was hearing me or not. If he was he didn't let me know.

We placed the heart monitor on the dead man and turned it on. What I saw surprised me. The monitor was showing a normal heart rhythm. I stared at the man in disbelief. I again searched for a pulse, and this time I felt the familiar push against my fingers. A few seconds later the man started to breathe, and then to moan and groan. I couldn't believe what I was seeing. His groans turned into words, and he asked me had what happened. I didn't know what to say to him. I was completely shocked. I didn't even answer his question. It only took a couple of seconds before my training kicked back in and I began to prepare him for a trip to the hospital. He looked at me and said he felt fine and didn't need to go to the hospital. I looked at him in disbelief and told him that he was dead a few minutes ago so staying home wasn't going to be an option.

We lifted the man onto our stretcher and loaded him into the rescue. By the time we arrived at the hospital, all of his vital signs were normal, and he had no complaints. Later we found out that he had suffered a tear in his aorta, and the hospital staff had rushed him up to surgery. People who suffer tears in their aorta typically bleed and die in a minute or two. The man's aorta had ruptured at home, and he had bled out. He was hopelessly dead, and yet God brought him back to life!

As I considered the entire situation, I began to understand the magnitude of what God did. I had just witnessed a resurrection from the dead! I couldn't deny it. I had stepped out in faith, and God had delivered. I spent some time following this incident just standing in awe and praising God as my faith in His power grew. My "faith well" was filling up.

Drowning

A couple of weeks later came my second opportunity to step out in faith. I was just sitting down for lunch when the station tones rang signaling an emergency. We were dispatched to a drowning with CPR in progress. The call was not in our immediate area, and it took us about ten minutes to get to the scene. The rescue team that normally handled that area was busy with another emergency.

As we sped to the scene, I quietly prayed against death and asked God for a miracle, but with the extended response time I wasn't expecting one. Even though I had seen God raise the dead there was still unbelief in my heart. I thought that maybe it was a one-time thing. I was beginning to understand that God is who He says He is but with only one experience my confidence was pretty shaky. I heard that terrible voice in my ear saying, *"God may have done it once but He won't do it again. Don't even bother praying."*

When I first saw the woman, I thought, *"Lord, this is a big one."* She looked awful. She reminded me of the story of Lazarus being dead for days. The woman's husband had found her in the pool and didn't know how long she had been there. She was pale and very cold. She had been under water for a significant amount of time. I was having trouble looking past what my eyes saw in the natural, and it was stunting my faith. I didn't think there was any hope at all.

We hooked the woman up to the heart monitor, and it confirmed death by showing a flat line. When a person's heart stops beating, there are different rhythms we can see on the heart monitor. A flat line is the worst one possible. It's so bad that, when we see it, we don't even try to shock the heart because it won't respond to that kind of treatment.

It's unsettling how doubt in the ability of God to work miracles slides in so easily. So many times what we see and know in the natural can destroy our faith in God's supernatural ability. I had said many times before that nothing is too big for God, but when faced with this seemingly hopeless situation I thought, *"This is too big."* But as I was getting the IV supplies out to try my best, I heard the soft voice of the Holy Spirit say, *"Just wait and see what I can do."* It was as if the voice brought a wave of peace and faith. It was enough to uncover some hope in the power of God. I took a moment to quietly pray against death and ask God to heal the woman. There was a lot of commotion around me so I don't think anyone heard me pray. Even though I had heard the soft voice of God I still felt like I was running on faith fumes. I could only half-heartedly check for a pulse. I almost fell over backwards in surprise when a soft thud hit my fingers. I looked at my partner and said in shock, "I have a pulse." He looked at me in disbelief and said, "What?" We worked very quickly getting her ready for transport to the hospital. By the time we got the woman into a hospital room, all of her vital signs were normal and I was still trying to wrap my mind around what had just happened.

I was beginning to understand something important. God has a habit of making the impossible completely possible. God was beginning to stack up some incredible testimonies in my life and as a result, a foundation of faith was being built in my heart. My position that God can do anything was moving from just an intellectual principle to a heart principle, and it was changing my life. I was seeing His hand in ways I never thought I would.

What's a Normal Christian Experience?

Jesus tells us to heal the sick and raise the dead (Matt. 10:8) but that wasn't part of my Christian experience. Jesus sent out seventy-two "unknowns" and told them to heal the sick (Luke 10:1-23) but that wasn't part of my Christian experience. Jesus, Paul, Elijah, Elisha, and Peter raised the dead (Acts 9:36-42, 20:9-12; Luke 7:13-15; 2 Kings 4:35; 1 Kings 17:17-24) but that wasn't a part of my Christian experience. Jesus told us that we would do the same things that He did and even greater things (John 14:12) but that wasn't a part of my Christian experience. I wasn't living the kind of life Jesus commissioned His followers to live. I was dead in my walk with Him. But God exposed my lukewarm existence and began to teach me what a normal Christian walk *should* look like. God transformed me with His resurrection power (Phil. 3:10), exposing the areas of my heart that were held captive by our adversary. Jesus set me free from a life of captivity and prepared me for a life of incredible freedom.

My primary passion in life is to know Jesus "in the power of the resurrection and in the fellowship of His sufferings, becoming like Him..." (Philippians 3:10). It is my desire to be more like Him every day. I only look to Jesus as the model for my life. What He did and what He taught His followers to do is what this book is all about. My journey might not look like yours, and that's OK. Paul said, follow me, even as I follow Christ (1 Corinthians 11:1). Your life needs to be like His and not mine. God wants to use us all in unique ways. Jesus modeled every single facet of ministry and each of us can represent a different part of that. If we want to be like Him we must be willing to say "yes."

There are many more powerful testimonies in the pages ahead. Many are experiences from my own life but there are also testimonies from other ordinary people who have said, "yes" to the Lord. I want you to understand that there is no such thing as a "SuperChristian." The commission of Jesus is for everyone who believes, not just some. By the end of this book my desire is that you will understand the hope to which He has called you, that the riches of His glorious inheritance are for you, His incomparably great power is in you, and that the great power in you is the same power He used to raise Christ from the dead (Eph. 1:18-21). I used to believe the lie that the miraculous power of God was only for a special few. I want you to understand how I came to know the truth, but first we need a little background.

The Beginning

I am the son of a pastor. I know what you're thinking: *"Oh this guy was a terrible kid."* Pastors' kids have quite a reputation for rebellion. I was not overly rebellious growing up, but I was not very spiritually minded. I did not read my Bible much, and I had no devotional life. My "quiet time" was done simultaneously with sleeping. God by osmosis was my theology. The fact that I didn't "sow wild oats" was not because I was taking a stand for righteousness, but because of my fear of rejection. To go out and party, I would have had to try to become friends with the "cool" crowd, and I did not want to put myself out there. I didn't like myself very much, and I wasn't interested in giving people a chance to reject me.

My exposure to the Lord was very laid back and gentle. I grew up in church, but my parents never tried to shove the Bible or Christianity down my throat. I remember my first experience with prayer. I was very young, and I was having the same nightmare over and over again. I wanted as many lights on in my room as possible, which frustrated my parents. One night after I had the nightmare, I got out of bed and braved the treacherous "dead-man's-stairs" to get downstairs to my parents. (My two sisters and I had all fallen down those stairs at least twice each.) My parents asked me if I wanted to pray, and I said yes. So we prayed. I never had that nightmare again.

The first church I remember being a part of was the first one that hired my dad as a senior pastor. My dad was a great pastor and an excellent teacher. Our church did not have a band, lights and smoke, but it was not overly traditional either.

I don't remember the Holy Spirit ever being dismissed in that first church. But I also don't remember people moving in the freedom of the Holy Spirit as outlined in 1 Corinthians 12 and 14. My dad never taught that the outward expressions of the gifts of the Spirit are not of God. We just simply did not operate in that way.

My dad pastored that church for ten years. Toward the end of our time there, when I was fifteen, I began to attend a community youth group. My older sister had gone a few times and loved it. She really wanted my younger sister and me to go with her.

This youth group was of no specific denomination and was open to whoever wanted to come and worship the Lord. There was a time of worship and ministry, and then someone would present a message.

As I look back, the fact that it was not the same person with a message each week was beautiful. There were a couple of weeks that I was able to get up and speak whatever God gave me to speak. It was a true picture of the body of Christ ministering to the body of Christ.

During the praise and worship time, there were kids of all ages ministering to each other. There was prophetic prayer and ministry, kids falling to their knees under the weight of the Holy Spirit, kids breaking down into tears, and kids discovering the real love of God for the first time. Were there some fakers in the crowd? I'm sure there were some. I remember praying for a kid around my age, and he fell down. I was sure it was an act, so I got down on the floor and told him, "If that was not of God and it was all you, stand up right now and receive what God really has for you." He slowly cracked his eye open. Realizing that I was not joking, he awkwardly stood up.

Despite the occasional "faker," there were real displays of the power of God every week. Teenagers were ministering to teenagers. People were healed emotionally and physically. Kids were getting saved, and the love of the Lord was heavy in the air.

I was excited about the Spirit of God moving in our youth group, and I became even more excited as I learned that God loves to move powerfully among His people. One night I felt that I was being drawn to the prophetic gift and the gift of speaking in tongues. I found one of the leaders and asked him to pray that God would give me the gift of prophecy and of tongues. That was an amazing night. God answered that prayer, and that night He even spoke to me in a dream. The reality that someone as big as God would take the time to speak to someone like me showed me that God loved me far beyond my ability to ever fully understand. That night I began to walk a road of maturing in the gifts of God—a road I am still walking today.

I attended the community youth group for about two years until my dad felt that God was asking him to move on to another phase of ministry. Just before my senior year of high school, we moved from Northeast Ohio to Sarasota, Florida, where my dad took a pastor position at another church.

The next eight years of my life were an incredibly long season. I call it my Lukewarm Era. These years were full of great joy and great pain. These were the years in which I graduated from college, married a beautiful woman, started a career as a firefighter, had a son, went to paramedic school, had a daughter, bought and sold our first house, lived with my in-laws for a year, and built and moved into a new house.

But these were also the years in which I struggled with addiction, saw my family ripped apart by false accusations, was out of relationship with my parents for three years, realized marriage was not all I thought it would be, felt like an inadequate father and husband, shut down emotionally, and just plain hated myself.

When this season ended, all of these painful things began to have happy endings, and it is only because of the miraculous power of God. I am no longer an addict, my family has been reconciled, I am very close to both of my parents, I began to "feel" again, my broken heart is being healed, my marriage now is better than I ever hoped it could be, and I realize that with God, I am adequate. He approved me when he created me, and now I love what He created.

But during those eight long years my whole existence was lukewarm. God and church were not very important. I loved God, but making a stand for righteousness was just not an interest. My wife, Kara, was always nagging me about doing my devotions or spending quiet time with God. She desperately wanted me to rise up and be the spiritual head of the house. But all I was interested in was finding out how I could get back to where I was spiritually when I was involved in that community youth group, and I didn't know how to get there. I was lost. I missed ministering to people. I could remember and feel the passion inside of me for people. But I was involved in a church that didn't practice the gifts of the Holy Spirit, and there was nowhere else around that I knew of where I could go and minister in the way that I used to. It is horrible to realize that you used to have something, but somewhere you lost it, and you don't know how to get it back.

So I just walked through life in the status quo. I read my Bible every now and then. I went to a Promise Keepers event. I went to some Bible studies and small groups with Kara. I was just going through the motions. I had grown stagnant. I had no relationship with God, and when you don't have relationship with God, existence is sad and empty. That would all change late one morning.

My Road to Damascus

My encounter with the Lord came about a week after I had taken a spiritual gifts test as part of the process of becoming a member of the church we were attending. I had taken those kinds of tests before, so I was just going through the motions. After the test, the facilitator asked for a show of hands as he said each gift of the Spirit. When he said, "Prophet," I raised my hand along with only one other person, the pastor. Only two in that big room full of people. It was shocking to me.

After the meeting, a woman whom I didn't recognize told me that she had something she was supposed to give me. I was very hungry at the time, so I was hoping it was some kind of food item or gift certificate. She told me that she had a set of CDs that God told her to give to me, a teaching series by Mike Bickle called *Encountering Jesus.*

I started listening to them the next morning when I got on the road to clean pools (I owned a pool-cleaning business). It was about a forty-five minute drive to my commercial accounts. I pulled into the parking lot of the apartment complex where my first pools were located. What happened next was strange, terrifying, and absolutely amazing. Mike Bickle had just started telling an amazing story of a man prophesying a comet in 1983, which was a sign that He was going to do what He told Mike He would. Something began to happen inside of me. It felt a little like after you drink an energy drink and the caffeine starts to run through your body, although I had not had an energy drink or any coffee that morning. I started to feel very jittery, and there was an overwhelming rush throughout my entire body. It started at my feet and ran up and into my head. I stumbled to the back of my truck to see if there was a chlorine leak, as I thought I might be suffering from some kind of chemical exposure. But there was no leak.

The feeling in my body intensified, and I felt like I might float off of the ground. Then the floating sensation minimized, and it seemed that all of the overwhelming sensation was focused directly on my heart. I felt like there was something pouring into me. I thought I was going to explode. I began to shake and sweat. I could not control it.

As the physical sensation was taking hold of my body, what I was experiencing in my spirit and soul was completely different. From the moment the sensation started, I was overcome with a feeling of peace even though it felt like my body was experiencing major trauma. Peace and love flooded my entire being along with the sense that I was in the presence of something more powerful than I had ever known. As it washed over me, I got a glimpse of the majesty and sheer power of the presence of the Almighty God. Even just this "glimpse" was enough to put me on my face moaning. There was a release of joy into my inner being and a sense of great purpose. God was showing me just how small I was in myself, but at the same time letting me know that He thought the world of me. He showed me that I was worth everything to him. I heard the voice of God speak to my heart saying, *"It is time for you. I am calling you out."* I had no idea what that meant, but I felt it resonate deep within my soul.

The experience was incredible. I called Kara as soon as I was able to compose myself, and told her what happened. I was talking very fast, totally freaking her out—especially when I told her that God just commissioned me for something, and I had no idea what it was or even where it was. I couldn't explain what had just happened, but I knew that my life was never going to be the same again. I had thought I had been on a journey with the Lord for twenty-six years but in a moment had discovered that my journey was just beginning.

Questions for Thought

- What does your "Christian experience" look like? Does it seem to line up with the life of Jesus and how He tells us to live, or does it seem to line up with something else? Do you want your life to line up with how Jesus lived?

- How does it make you feel to consider that God wants to

use you, an ordinary person, to perform miracles, signs and wonders? How could believing this change your life? How could it change the lives of everyone around you?

- Think about a time when you felt God might have been asking you to step out in faith in a certain way that made you uncomfortable. Did you do it? Why or why not?

- Consider what you have learned about God, the Holy Spirit and the church. Do your beliefs give you the freedom to operate in the commission Jesus gave us and in the capacity of Ephesians 1:18-21?

CHAPTER 2

THE DRAMA CONTINUES

"Hope is like the sun, which, as we journey toward it, casts the shadow of our burden behind us." – Samuel Smiles

A Powerful Morning

It was early, and I had just arrived at my station. Before I could even pour some coffee down my throat, the tones went off, and we were speeding away. We had been dispatched to a cardiac arrest. Any call can be difficult first thing in the morning, but especially a cardiac arrest. I shook off any remaining cobwebs and began to quietly battle against death in prayer. I asked the Lord to work another miracle. I was getting more and more comfortable praying on the way to calls, and I was doing it with more faith than ever. I was beginning to expect great things.

When we arrived on the scene, we found a young girl frantically attempting CPR on her unconscious mother. My partner hastily escorted the girl out of the room, and I rapidly checked the patient to find that she was not breathing and did not have a pulse. Finding the patient this way didn't concern me as much as it did in the past. The hopelessness I used to feel didn't seem to be a part of me anymore. In its place was a new confidence and faith in the ability of God to perform the impossible.

While I was waiting for the rest of my crew to come in with the equipment, I resumed CPR and continued the spiritual battle against death. I had already seen God do miracles, and I knew He could do another. I was focusing more on the ability of God rather than on what I saw in the natural. Doubt was losing ground in my life.

As we applied the heart monitor and oxygen to the woman, I continued to quietly pray against death and spoke healing in the name of Jesus. The heart monitor showed a flat-line rhythm. But this time I didn't lose hope. I continued to work and pray with an expectation that God was going to do something miraculous. The voice that used to tell me that God wasn't with me had become inaudible. The only voice I could hear was the voice of God telling me that He was with me and to keep working.

I had just finished starting an IV when a member of my crew asked me excitedly if there was a pulse. I looked at my partner and then at the heart monitor. My heart leapt when I saw a normal rhythm floating across the heart monitor. I quickly checked for a pulse and I felt it silently assuring me that once again God had poured out His grace and mercy in a miraculous way. My heart swelled in the miraculous display of love and mercy God poured out onto this woman and her family. I thanked God as we rapidly loaded the formerly dead patient into our rescue and sped toward the hospital.

We had arrived on a scene full of death and sorrow. God had asked for a little faith in His ability, and the result was victory. Instead of giving death to the emergency room doctors, we passed on life. I left the hospital in awe of how God was using an ordinary person like me in such awesome ways. I was realizing that I didn't have to be "special" to be used by God. I just had to be willing and understand a few things. First, I had to understand who I was in Christ and who He was in me. Second, I had to have faith that God is who He says He is and can do what He says He can do. Third, I had to understand the power and authority made available to me by Jesus (Luke 10:19) and how to exercise that power and authority. I'll share more about these things later.

30

Uh-Oh!

It was late, and things were quiet at the fire station. I was in bed trying to get some sleep before the next call. I felt like I had just closed my eyes, when the emergency tones blasted. Less than a minute later, we were speeding toward a person who was reportedly having trouble breathing.

We arrived on the scene, where my gut was telling me that this was more than just a minor incident, so we worked with a sense of urgency. My partner and I helped the woman onto our stretcher, and we loaded her into the rescue. I gave her the appropriate medicine for her condition, and she told me she was getting some relief. My partner hooked her up to the heart monitor, and I turned my head to see what it was showing. What I saw caused me some concern. The heart was beating abnormally, and it was beating too quickly. It needed to be corrected. I asked God to help and got out the appropriate medicine. I asked the woman if her heart had ever been abnormal before, and she told me that she didn't think it had. I was concerned but not overly so. The particular condition our patient had was common and is usually easy to correct.

I administered the medicine and watched the heart monitor for any changes. I didn't have to wait very long as the monitor showed the patient's heart slowing down to normal. I breathed relief, but before I could relax I was hit by a jolt of anxiety caused by what I saw next. The heart was now slower than normal and was getting even slower. I held my breath and gripped the sides of my seat as I watched the heart rate get slower and slower—and then stop altogether.

All of the blood in my head drained, and my heart was in my throat as the monitor showed the dreaded flat line. The woman was dead. I reached for the tools I needed and found my voice. I prayed against death and destruction and prayed for another miracle in the name of Jesus. I didn't know what was happening, but I knew God was bigger than whatever it was and that He could fix it.

Suddenly the monitor wasn't showing a flat line anymore. It was showing a thin, jagged line, which the monitor shows when the heart is quivering. It's still dead, but it will respond to electric shock.

I grabbed the equipment I needed to shock the patient's heart and looked again at the monitor. It had changed again and was now showing a heart that was quivering but also producing full beats. My mouth hung open as I tried to process what was happening and figure out what to do next. As it turned out, the only thing I had to do was watch because the monitor changed again just a few seconds later to reflect a normal heart rhythm. My partner and I exchanged looks of shock and disbelief.

I looked at the patient's face. Her eyes flickered open, and she groaned. She was taking full breaths through her dry mouth. She weakly asked what had happened. I told her that she was sick but that she was much better. I was too overwhelmed to say much more. My heart was rejoicing as once again the power of God was on full display. We took her to the hospital alive and well. All of her vitals were stable and she was feeling fine. Death had been defeated, and a powerful testimony of the resurrection power of Jesus Christ went out to forcefully advance His kingdom.

A Few Things to Address…

I need to take a moment here to address a couple of things before we move on. The first is about my partners at work. I work with many different people with many different beliefs. I have run into only a few who share my beliefs and I don't work with them very often. I have not taken the time to write about my partners' reactions because, frankly, there is nothing to write about. There have not been any dramatic conversions or any further discussions based on what I am doing on calls. If anyone has been aware of me praying over patients in the previous stories (and the stories ahead) they have not let me know. I work with good people but they are people who are more likely to credit medicine and individual skill than to recognize the hand of God at work.

The second thing to address is whether there has been any continued interaction with the patients mentioned to whom something miraculous happened. The vast majority of the time the only interaction I will ever have with a patient is the time it takes to transport them to the hospital. Due to privacy and logistical issues, I am not able to provide any information about where they are now and how they are. I just don't know. But I do know that in the short time I was with these people God did some truly amazing things. I believe with absolute certainty that every testimony mentioned in this book is the result of miraculous intervention from God! I look forward to sharing many more experiences with you but first we need a little more background into my life.

The Beginning Continued

The day God met me in my Blazer changed my life, and the following year can be divided into seasons. I received a crash course in a handful of different areas. The first season was marked by a special focus on the prophetic.

When I was involved in the community youth group, I had some experience praying for people prophetically, specifically with words of knowledge. But it had been a very long time since that youth group, and I hadn't been able to hear the voice of God since then. I had not prophesied to anyone and had hardly even prayed for anyone since that time eight years earlier.

Many things changed in my life after my Blazer experience. I began to get up early and spend at least an hour every day in prayer and reading the Bible. I began fasting two days a week. I began to journal everything that I was hearing God speak. My corporate worship experience underwent an extreme makeover. My box of inhibitions during worship exploded, and I began to sing and clap loudly, raise my hands, jump, dance, pray out loud during worship, speak in tongues, and make trips to the altar, where I fell to my knees before the Lord. It was wonderful and felt very freeing. I freaked a lot of people out, including Kara, but I had more freedom in my life than I had ever known. You have to understand that I was a firefighter who had turned off all emotions and cared about my image more than anything else.

It was during the quiet times and times when I was just thinking about God that He began to teach me how to hear His voice. He began to awaken the prophetic gift in me and to speak to me about the church we attended. It was all good and encouraging. There was a small group of people who spent time in prayer every Sunday morning. I joined them. We prayed for the church and the city. God confirmed many of the things He spoke to me in private as I prayed with these people. One woman in particular would often pray out loud what God had spoken to me in private. There were many times that I would share a "word" (prophecy), and she would confirm it by showing me that God had spoken the same thing to her earlier that week. Confirmation was very important to me as I learned to hear the voice of God, and it encouraged me greatly.

I remember one story in particular; it was one of the first big confirmations that God gave me. I was spending some time in prayer when God spoke and said that our church was called to be a house of prayer. I asked, "Lord, who is going to facilitate this?" The next thing I heard was the name of a man in our church. I called one of the people I prayed with and asked her what I should do. She told me that if I felt that it was God's timing for this man to know, then I should call him and tell him. I did feel like God was saying that it was OK to call him, so I did. He answered the phone, and after some small talk, I told him that I felt God was calling him to be a big part of prayer in our church. His response was that lately he had been feeling a passion for prayer and was unsure if it was from God or not. Wow! God had used me to speak into this man's life, and it was amazing. God provided confirmation, and I was encouraged.

I have discovered that many times God will use confirmation to teach us. However, He will also use our mistakes. I have learned some valuable lessons the hard way. One of the first mistakes I made was in the realm of interpretation. Our church had been meeting in a building we didn't own, and plans were in motion to build our own church home. The new building was going to cost a few million dollars, and there was a lot of concern over the finances. God spoke to me and told me that the church would have what it needed by a specific date. I was moved by what I knew the church needed, and I interpreted the meaning to be that the church would have the money for the building. I told fewer than five people about this, including the pastor. I told them I wasn't sure, and I asked them all to pray about it with me. Unfortunately there were some people who took my interpretation as "gospel." The date came and went, and there was no money. God fulfilled that word in a different and wonderful way, but it wasn't the way I had interpreted it. The pastor extended grace and forgiveness to me, but some false accusations began circulating about me. It hurt me, and I had no defense. I got it wrong. I am human. God taught me several very important things through this.

- Just because God speaks a word to you doesn't mean you are the one that's supposed to interpret it.

- If you present people with a word from God, there will be some who don't test it in prayer, but take it as truth, so speak with caution.

- Satan hates the prophetic, and when it is in operation, he will stir up people against it.

So there I was—a young man who'd had a dramatic experience. I was learning to hear from God prophetically by getting it right sometimes and messing things up other times. I was getting more and more comfortable speaking out when I heard from God, yet I only felt slightly more mature in the gifts. God had me on a fast track. It was trial by fire. Sink or swim. Kara stood by me, but was unsure of what I was getting into. I was still so young and felt like there was a huge mountain of knowledge God had yet to teach me about the prophetic. Just the little that he had taught me so far was making my relationships with people very different and more difficult. Kara and I had no idea how much more uncomfortable things would become for us.

Lions and Tigers and Demons. Huh?

I knew that there was a lot more that God wanted to teach me regarding the prophetic. I began looking for a local mentor who operated in the prophetic gift and could teach me. My search led me to Richard Mull. The only things I knew were that he wrote a book called *The Jesus Training Manual* and that it was important that I meet him. I got a hold of his audio book and listened to some of it before I met him. I called Richard and told him who I was and that I was looking for someone who operated in the prophetic to help me with some questions. He agreed to meet with me. We met at a Cuban café. I got there first and ordered coffee. I took my seat and waited. A few minutes later Richard walked in and sat down. We introduced ourselves, and I asked him if he was going to get anything to eat. He said no because he was fasting. I was also fasting at that time. Great! We had at least one thing in common. Then he said he was going to get some juice because he didn't drink coffee while fasting. *"La-di-da. Mr. Spiritual, here,"* I thought as I took a big sip of my coffee.

I could tell right away that I liked this man, though. He was sincere and genuine. I asked him questions, and he answered the best that he could. I told him about some mistakes I had made, and he offered encouragement. There was a connection. The things this guy was saying were resonating deep in my soul. I knew that God had ordained the meeting.

Our meeting came to a close, and he prayed for me. I could tell that I had just made a friend and that he was going to be very important in my life. He told me about a conference coming up that was based on another of his books, *Lord Heal Me*. I said that I would try and make it, and we parted ways.

I continued to listen to his audio book. As I was listening, I felt the next season begin to come upon me. In his book, Richard shared about healing the sick, casting out demons, and preaching the gospel. He also told how deliverance can be connected to healing. The information on casting out demons, deliverance and healing was catching most of my attention.

I had never been very uncomfortable with the issue of demons. I had never been in the "demons don't have any effect on Christians" camp but I had never had any strong theology on the issue either. When it came to demons and Christians and how they interact, all I had was a big question mark. But I began to gain a more Biblical understanding and theology as I listened to Richard's book. Everything that he was saying was making sense and resonating in my soul as truth. It was lining up with scripture. I wanted to know more.

I went to see my pastor to discuss some questions I was having about demons. He gave me a book by Peter Horrobin called *Healing Through Deliverance Volume 1*. This was an introduction into the area of deliverance. Biblical, grounded, and very well written, it was one of the most important tools God used to give me some understanding in the area of deliverance. During this time of reading and praying and wanting to know more, I felt the Holy Spirit tugging on my spirit. I knew that I was supposed to be learning about demons and deliverance and that God was going to teach me.

I decided to go to Richard Mull's conference. I was excited to see what God was going to do. On the second day, Richard was telling stories about how he was ministering to all sorts of people and was seeing the power of God change their lives. He told stories of God revealing hurts and pain in people's lives. As they understood the pain, allowed God to heal their broken hearts, and repented of sin, God healed them emotionally and physically. He had stories about how demons would begin to manifest when he was teaching. He would go over to the person, take authority over the spirit, and cast it out. This man was seeing the power of God operate in people's lives every day. He was walking in the authority that Christ has given to all of us, and I wanted to know how to do that. I didn't want the enemy to rule in my life anymore. I was getting excited and a little emotional. I felt a clear calling into the ministry of deliverance.

At the next break, I walked up to Richard and shook his hand. I hadn't seen him in about a month, so I was not sure if he would remember me, but he did. His handshake was warm and sincere. I told him I felt that I should be doing what he was talking about. I told him I felt like I wanted to be a part of his ministry. He told me that before they allowed someone to minister to others, that person first had to be ministered to.

Let me take a moment to explain "ministry." There are many people who react very badly to the word "deliverance." The ministry that Richard Mull founded, Operation Light Force, uses the word "discipleship" instead of "deliverance." "Ministry" does not include people jumping up and down yelling and screaming at demons. People who come in for help are not hit on the head with a Bible or dunked in "holy water." They do not leave with a crucifix plastered to their forehead. The point is that "deliverance" is probably not what you think. We believe that the source of our problems is not just spiritual, but also emotional. We all have emotional wounds and scars, and if you go to a ministry where all they do is cast out demons, you are missing half of the battle. Likewise if you go to a psychologist or therapist and all they do is address the emotional pain and wounds but never take authority over the demonic influence, you are also missing half of the battle. We have found that demons ride the coattails of emotional wounds. For example, our significant other dumps us. The emotional pain in that is rejection amongst other things. Some of the demons that use this event to gain access to our hearts are bitterness, unforgiveness, self-rejection, and self-hatred. Ministry consists of allowing God to heal the emotional pain of rejection by talking about it, exploring it and allowing God to heal the broken heart. Ministry also includes breaking the power of the demonic influence of bitterness and self-hate, casting them out of our lives and learning to walk in freedom. We need both facets to be free.

Before I went to receive ministry, I didn't have a very good understanding of what it would involve, but I knew I was supposed to walk this path. The day of my appointment came, and I was nervous. I had no idea what was going to happen, but I did know that I was going to get an hour and a half to talk about myself. I have discovered that it is a wonderful thing when someone listens to your babbles for a while. Who doesn't like to talk about themselves? I was going to be the most important person for a whole ninety minutes!

On my way to the appointment, I realized that even though I did not know what was going to happen, I was ready for God to do whatever he wanted to do. It took two appointments for God to tear down the emotional walls that I had built over the previous eight years. A large part of the emotional wall was the result of a particular trauma. Someone close to me that I cared about accused me of some horrific things that weren't true. This person's false accusations had shattered other relationships that were very important to me. I stuffed all of the pain, emotions and anger so deep that I couldn't feel anything relating to this trauma. One of the ministers with me asked me if I was angry as I shared the event with them. I told her "No" and I meant it. But the truth of my condition was addressed. I saw that in order to heal I was going to have to feel the pain. God can't heal pain we refuse to recognize. I was led to ask God to reconnect my emotions and suddenly I felt a wail form deep within me, with an intensity far beyond my experience. It terrified me as it grew and overtook me. It was eight years of repressed emotion. I knew the wail was going to exit through my mouth, and I was sure the building was going to come apart. I tried my best to keep things under some sort of control, but my emotional dam burst. As I bent over at the waist, I groaned with such intensity I thought my head was going to explode. I was being delivered from significant demonic influence and captivity.

I began to feel emotions for what seemed like the first time. That was to be a recurring theme for me during that season. Experiencing things for what seems to be the first time is one of the fruits of God's healing. Feeling emotions for the first time in eight years is like being born again. I was holding onto every emotion. It was wonderful; I was alive again!

That was only the first of many wounds God began to heal in me. Over the following months, God taught me many things. I saw demons manifest in Christians, and I cast them out in Jesus' name (I'll share more about the interaction between Christians and demons later). I learned much about the occult and how subtle it is. I saw God break hard men and women. I saw the power of God's love in action. This was an extended season for me compared to the others. God had much to heal in me and teach me about spiritual warfare.

Some of the most important things God healed in me came over the course of my one and only (God willing!) forty-day fast. Have you ever thought about fasting that long? I had heard of it and knew enough to know that I wanted no part of it. I thought things like that were only for super spiritual people. Enter our friends, Joey and Nikki.

My wife Kara wife met Nikki at the gym and wanted me to meet her and her husband. After a few weeks of hounding, we made plans to get together for lunch. The day came, and when we sat down to eat at their house, Joey began to pray over the food. At least that's what I thought he was going to do; I'm sure he mentioned the food in there somewhere. His praying was soft at first and then got louder and more passionate. He began praying words like "Spirit of God" and asking for revelation and words. He was almost wailing at certain points. I can't remember exactly where Nikki jumped in, but it was seamless. Only when she jumped in, it was in tongues! I sat there with my mouth half open thinking, "Wow! I thought we were going to eat, not start a revival!" I did know one thing: this was going to be the most blessed food I was ever going to eat.

For some reason they stopped; maybe because ten minutes is way too long to bless food. But after we ate and drank some coffee, the Holy Spirit came upon them, and they began to prophecy over me. They spoke a word over me that I had heard before; they told me that God was raising me up to be a general in His army. It was exactly what a man with a prophetic anointing had told me ten years earlier. That was some serious confirmation! They also

ten years earlier. That was some serious confirmation! They also told me that God was going to get up close and personal for me. It was at that moment God spoke to my spirit and told me to start a forty-day fast and that I wasn't going to come out of it the way I would go in. How true that was.

During those forty days, God healed some very important things in me. He healed and set me free from self-hatred. I experienced the perfect love of God, and Satan was no longer able to steal it. I had forgiven myself, and for the first time I was trusting and relying on God's love. He healed me from fear. I was free from fear, worry, stress, and anxiety for the first time in my life. I experienced how perfect love casts out fear (1 John 4:18). God took me through many judgments I had made about people and healed the bitterness that had flowed out of them. I began walking in love and compassion for people. And He delivered me from a religious spirit that had me trying to please God with my religious works. I came out of those forty days a totally different person. It was amazing. Those healings signaled the closing of that season, and the focus changed again.

My Season of Prophecy. Again.

It had been about nine months since my Blazer encounter. I heard about a couple offering a prophetic class and decided to attend. It was about learning to hear the voice of God. It was a safe place to listen and speak. There were about twenty people who would come, and we would participate in exercises in which we would speak out loud what we heard God speaking to each of us.

This class was amazing. God grew and matured me in the prophetic over the month or two that followed. I did some things right, and I did some things wrong. When I messed up, God corrected me, and I learned from the experience. I came away really knowing what the voice of God sounds like. Today when God speaks something to me, I know it's Him, and I speak it boldly. Of course I know that I am going to get it wrong at times. I am human, and I will never be finished growing and maturing in the gifts God has given me. But God's plan for me during that season was to make me more confident in Him and to make me a "man" in the spiritual sense. The fear that had grown a root in me because of the misinterpretation of the church money way back was gone, and I felt better equipped than I ever had. Retrospect is a funny thing. If I had known why God wanted me to be bold, I may have run.

Questions For Thought

- Do you feel like you're making progress in your journey with God, or do you seem to be at a standstill?

- What are your beliefs about deliverance? Do they line up with scripture?

- What are you beliefs about the spiritual gifts like prophecy, tongues and healing? Do your beliefs line up with scripture?

- I have found that many times our understanding of God comes from the teachings of others (pastors and other spiritual authorities) and we never bother to search for ourselves. I encourage you to take your beliefs from questions two and three and find support in the Bible. You might be surprised by what you find or don't find.

- God radically transformed my heart and my life when I finally surrendered every piece of it to Him. Are you ready to surrender every piece of your heart and life to God?

CHAPTER 3

A WORD IN DUE SEASON

"It is wonderful what miracles God works in wills that are utterly surrendered to Him. He turns hard things into easy, and bitter things into sweet. It is not that He puts easy things in the place of the hard, but He actually changes the hard thing into an easy one."
– Hannah Whitall Smith

Some of the scariest people to minister to are our co-workers. Unlike the random people we meet on the street, we have to see our co-workers all the time. That means that if we extend ourselves at work and are dismissed, we have to deal with the consequences as long as we are working with them. There is a lot of "fear of rejection" in that scenario. We all want to be liked, but not everything God gives us to speak is a nice, comfortable word. While much of the time the Lord wants to use us to comfort, encourage, and exhort others (1 Cor. 14:3), sometimes He wants us to correct others. That can make ministering to anyone, much less co-workers, a very uncomfortable thing, so most of the time we just keep our mouths shut and ignore the tugging on our spirits.

I had just arrived at work, and I was relieving a young woman whom I had never met before. As she was briefing me on the condition of the rescue, I felt the familiar tug of the Holy Spirit and the glory of God weighed on my heart. This is how the Lord tells me that it's time to minister in some way. The Lord began to speak to my heart and told me that this young woman was a believer. So I said to her, "You're a believer, aren't you?" She said, "Yes," and I proceeded to speak to her the words God was laying on my heart. The words were encouraging and full of love. They spoke about what God thought of her and how much He loved her. They spoke into some conditions in her home and the way she had been feeling at work. The words spoke to the condition of her heart and some of the things God wanted to do in her and around her. I watched as she began to get very emotional as the Lord ministered to her heart. Her eyes were wide and full of life as the Lord breathed refreshment through her.

This encounter was especially memorable because those who know me know that I am not a morning person by any means. Yet there I was, speaking a prophetic word to a woman who I have never met first thing in the early morning. I'm barely functional most mornings, let alone in a state of awareness to be used by God. Praise God that He doesn't care if we think we are in an unusable state. He still wants to use us even when we think He can't.

What would have happened if I had kept my mouth shut and ignored the Lord? What if I had decided that I was too tired and stubbornly refused to be obedient? Would God have found someone else to be obedient and give her the word? He may have, but maybe not. She really needed to hear from the Lord that morning. That was a word for her in due season. As we begin to walk the journey with God, He will show us people who need Him. Take great courage, and be obedient because that person's life might depend on it.

Delivered

A day before my scheduled work day, I got a phone call telling me that I would be working at a different station. The next morning I drove to my normal station to pick up my gear and then headed to the station I had been assigned to for the day. I was pretty annoyed because I don't like having to go work at other stations. It's a hassle to drag all of my gear and belongings along. However, I realized that if I was being sent to another station for the day, then God must have some reason for it. I began to ask Him why He was sending me somewhere else for the day.

I got my answer at about noon. We were called out to a person having some pain in his chest. As we arrived on the scene, I could see that we were in the bad part of town. We were called to help someone in an area known for drugs, shootings, and terrible living conditions. We entered the home and attended to the patient. After we gathered all of the information we needed, we loaded the patient onto the stretcher and placed him inside the rescue.

As my partner drove us to the hospital I looked at our patient. He was a middle-aged, hard-looking man. I could tell that he had been through some pretty rough stuff in his life. His clothes were pretty worn, and he looked like he hadn't slept in days. He looked like someone who was carrying a burden that was way too heavy. My heart began to pound as I felt the stirring of the Holy Spirit inside of me. I knew something was going to happen, but I didn't know what.

A couple of minutes had gone by when the man suddenly turned his head and said, "I have a weak heart." I said, "No you don't." He answered, "Says who?" I responded, "Says me right now!" After this interesting interaction, the man asked me if I was a Christian. I answered him by saying, "I am a follower of Jesus." He understood that and said, "OK." I took that opportunity to ask him about his experience with God. He looked at me and began to tell me about how he had run from God for twenty years. He told me that long ago God had called him to preach the word, and since then he had been like Jonah, resisting God's call on his life.

My heart broke as I listened to him tell me about some of the tragic things he had walked through. I asked him if he was ready to stop running. He said that he was, and there was sincerity in his voice. I asked him if there was anything he felt like he needed to repent of. He thought for a couple of seconds and emotionally told me that he didn't know how to forgive himself for the things that he had done. There it was! God was moving, and He was bringing the ministry of reconciliation straight into the back of my rescue. Satan had a hold on this man, but it was about to be broken.

I looked at the man and I asked him if he wanted to forgive himself right now. He said that he did. I began to lead him through a prayer of forgiveness. I led him to a certain point and then let him begin to forgive himself for specific things that had brought shame and guilt into his soul. He began listing things as tears filled his eyes. His voice grew stronger as he continued to forgive and I could see the chains falling off of his heart. Death and pain were leaving, and love, peace, and hope were being birthed. The power and presence of the Lord was all around us.

When he was finished, I led him in binding and casting out the spirits of self-hatred and unforgiveness. I didn't know what his experience with deliverance was, but I was doing what the Holy Spirit was telling me to do. After the demons were cast out, the prophetic word came through me. It was a beautiful word of love and encouragement. It was also a call to continued obedience and living a new life in righteousness. The Holy Spirit was touching the man's soul, and a peace came over him that he had never felt before.

As we arrived at the hospital I asked him how he felt. He told me that he felt free, and he smiled all the way into the emergency room. The chest pain was almost completely gone! That is what it means to take the light of God into the dark places and watch everything become light (Isa. 42:16). I don't know anything about what this man did from that day on, but I know that he was touched by God and set free in the back of a rescue. I pray that he continued to allow God to transform him into a new creation.

Breakthrough

It was just past lunchtime when we were dispatched to a person having a seizure. My partner and I climbed into the rescue and headed in the direction of the emergency. We arrived on scene and were met outside by the patient's girlfriend, who explained the patient's medical problems. We followed the woman into the home, and she directed us to where the patient, who we'll call Joe, was lying. He was awake, and answered all of my questions appropriately. The family was there and told us all about the seizure that they had just witnessed and how long seizures had been a problem for Joe. I assessed Joe and decided that he could stand on his own and walk over to our stretcher. We helped Joe to the stretcher and loaded him into the rescue. A short time later we were heading toward the hospital.

Joe was a very nice guy. We talked for a little while, just building a relationship. Joe's condition had been deteriorating over the previous couple of weeks, and he knew it. His countenance was heavy and dark as despair held him captive. In front of me was a man nearing the end of his life way too soon. As I looked at him, compassion filled my heart, and I felt the Holy Spirit begin to stir within me. The Holy Spirit began to speak to me and told me that Joe was being held prisoner by regret and failure in his life. I asked Joe if he had been reflecting over his life lately. He told me "no" and that he knew he was getting ready to die. I knew he wasn't telling the truth, so I asked him a different question. I asked him if he had any regrets. He said, "Of course, doesn't everyone?"

After that the Lord didn't give me anything else to say until we had placed Joe in the hospital bed in the emergency room. It was then that the Lord chose to stir powerfully inside of me. I asked Joe to look at me, and when I met his defeated eyes, I began to speak to Joe what I was hearing from God. I told Joe that God had used me many times to speak to people just like him. I told him that I felt like it was important for him to know that God still loved him.

It was at that moment that the prophetic word of the Lord came for Joe. I spoke the words the Lord gave me to speak, and as I did the Lord spoke and ministered healing into specific past regrets and failures. The Lord told Joe that he was not a failure, but a loved son of God. The Lord began to speak into and establish Joe's identity as an adopted son of God. The Lord addressed Joe's concerns for his family and regrets he had about his relationship with them. By that time Joe had reached his hand out for mine and was grasping it tightly. Tears were streaming down his face as the Lord used me to speak love and healing into his soul. As the word came to an end, the room filled with peace and love and the presence of our almighty Daddy.

47

I said good-bye to Joe and left the room. I was walking down the hall when Joe's nurse stopped me. She told me that she had heard me with Joe. I wasn't sure what to expect, and I was a little nervous, but she proceeded to tell me how awesome it was for her to see that happen. She asked me what faith I was. I told her that I was a follower of Jesus. She thanked me and told me that she was blessed by what God did for Joe. My heart was full as I walked out of the ER.

The Atheist

It was about noon on a very hot day at work. I sat down with my crew to eat lunch, but instead found myself heading out the door and into the rescue to help an elderly woman who wasn't feeling well. We arrived on the scene at an assisted-living facility, where a staff member directed us to the patient's room. I found an elderly woman sitting in a chair. We'll call her Sue. She told me how sick she felt. I assessed her and found that she possibly had an infection of some kind. Sue was very pleasant despite feeling so bad, and we built an instant rapport. After a few minutes we left the facility and entered the rescue. We prepared Sue for transport to the hospital, and in no time we were speeding away.

Sue and I began to talk, and I asked her if she wanted to me to pray for her. She said that I could if I wanted, but that she didn't believe in it. I was disappointed and a little mad. I thought to myself, "If she doesn't believe in it, then I'm not going to do it." The Holy Spirit spoke to me in that moment and told me to keep asking her questions about her life. The Lord gave me some pretty specific questions to ask, and by the time we arrived at the hospital, I had a pretty good idea why Sue didn't believe in God and prayer. Sue had experienced much tragic loss in her life. Many of her loved ones had died early and left her alone. In her experience God hadn't done anything good for her. She blamed Him for all the bad.

I took Sue into the emergency room and got her settled into the hospital bed. It was there that the Lord released me to begin to speak to her in a prophetic way. The message was about how

God grieved with her through her losses and how He saw her and viewed her as His daughter. The message was a love letter to a long-lost daughter, calling her home to His everlasting arms. Love filled the room and chased away doubt. As I spoke the words to Sue, her body position began to change. When I first began speaking the message, Sue was lying flat with her legs out. As the message concluded, Sue was lying on her side with her knees brought up almost to her chest as if she was being cradled. All she could do was look at me through tears and mouth the words "thank you." The look in her eyes told me that God had just touched something deep inside of her that she had tried carefully to hide. I smiled and said, "God bless you," then turned and left. Our God is truly an awesome God!

Love in Action

It was a rainy afternoon at station twelve, and we were called out to a person with a diabetic problem. We arrived on the scene and discovered a young girl who had been vomiting all morning. She explained to us how weak and sick she felt. As I talked with the family, they told me about how unstable she was. The young girl was more fragile than most elderly diabetics I have seen. She had been to a children's hospital, and they could not seem to get her blood sugar stabilized. She also had a number of other medical problems that made her feel horrible all of the time.

The girl didn't say a word as we moved her onto the stretcher and took her out to the rescue. Her veins were so poor that we could not start an IV. Even though she didn't open her eyes, I could see the heaviness, hopelessness, and despair on her. It was breaking my heart. She was breathing very hard trying to control the nausea and kept her eyes tightly shut. She was very weak. We headed for the hospital, and as we drove, the Lord began to speak to me. I was filled with compassion for this "daughter of the King," and I asked her if she wanted me to pray for her. There was no response for a couple of seconds, and then I saw her head slowly nod yes. She was still breathing pretty hard, and there was no peace in her body. I began to pray and delivered the words that God gave me for her. I also began to pray against different spirits of infirmities and diseases and cast them out in the name of Jesus. As I prayed, prophesied, and warred spiritually for the girl, she suddenly jerked a couple of times. The Lord showed me that things were changing for her, and I asked the Holy Spirit to fill her. Suddenly complete peace washed over her. Her breathing slowed to normal and became peaceful. The atmosphere around us transformed into peace as her eyes began to water.

The testimony here is not one of complete healing because I don't know if she was healed in that moment. What I do know is that this girl's perfect Daddy reached through all of her pain, suffering, infirmities, hopelessness, and despair and touched her heart. And through it, He definitely touched mine. The testimony here is the fiery, passionate love of God!

I hope that the testimonies I have shared here have helped you to understand that a word in the right season can dramatically change someone's life. Of course I am only talking about a word from the Lord being given to whomever He leads us to at any given time. When we walk in obedience to the Lord with a heart screaming, "Use me, Lord!" He will. It just takes a "Yes, Lord" instead of "No" or "Not right now" or "Use somebody else, God."

CHAPTER 4

FEAR NOT!

"Fear is born of Satan, and if we would only take time to think a moment we would see that everything Satan says is founded upon a falsehood." – A.B. Simpson

It was a dark and stormy night. The rain had slowed to a gentle sprinkle on the car windows as my dad pulled into a local gas station. I was about ten years old at the time. I clearly remember watching my dad pump gas into the car and then go into the gas station to pay. But I did not see him come back out and walk toward the car where my sister and I were waiting. When the front car door swung open, I spun around but could see only the back of a man. I didn't recognize my dad in the darkness, and I panicked. I threw off my seat belt and made it halfway out of the car before my he could get me to recognize who he was. I sat back terrified, but recovering.

Many of my earliest memories are laced with fear. I was a very fearful child. One of the fears that tormented me was the fear of being kidnapped. This fear kept me from staying home by myself, relaxing in public, and being completely comfortable with older people. I was also afraid of the weather. Living in Kansas exposed me to some pretty severe weather, and it had a lasting effect on me. My house was blown away by a tornado when I was seven, so that didn't help things to say the least. I was also afraid of the dark and had plenty of nightmares.

Some of you may think that fears are normal for children and that eventually they outgrow them. While I may have grown to a certain age at which I didn't fear being kidnapped, I didn't outgrow fear. The old fears just gave way to new ones. I became a teenager, and kids began to separate themselves into groups. The time when everyone was a friend to everyone came to an end, and I was presented with new problems. I began to fear rejection and abandonment. I began to fear other, bigger kids and the ability they had to inflict physical pain on me. I looked to sports to fit in and make something of myself, but I feared failure. I feared grades and not being smart enough. I feared girls because in my fuzzy perception, they ruled the balance of acceptance and rejection.

Even though I did better than average at sports and tried my best not to offend anyone, it wasn't enough to divert attention away from being an undersized teen who didn't curse, drink, or do drugs. As a result I was picked on and bullied. Now my fears were being realized. I was being rejected and abandoned. There was a loudspeaker in my brain telling me that I was worthless and insignificant. What I was hearing in my head was being reinforced in reality. I remember one particular incident as a freshman in high school. Everyone had been assembled in the gym, and I was sitting with my back toward a couple of my tormentors. A few minutes into the presentation, I felt something hitting my back. I ignored it and later discovered that they had been spitting on me. So there I was, just becoming a young man and having all of my fears validated. I felt that I had failed my teenage years. It wasn't all bad. There were plenty of good times. As I moved through high school, much of bullying faded away, but overall the fears remained.

Fast-forward some years. I am married, just starting a career as a firefighter/paramedic. I felt that I had gained some ground on the acceptance issue by getting married, but realized that I had picked up the horrible fear that my wife would leave or betray me. I feared losing my job, leading me to compromise my values and beliefs at work. I feared my superiors because they could fire me, leaving me poor and destitute. I feared my co-workers because they could reject me. I even feared my patients because they could complain and get me in trouble. I feared my children because they could expose me as a horrible and incompetent father. I feared money because it provided my security, and if I lost money, then I would lose my security. I feared sickness, disease, and death. Most of all I feared God, in an ungodly way, because I knew that if I really started to listen to Him, He would blow my world apart. I held my family at a distance because of fear and didn't have any emotionally intimate relationships. I lived a lifestyle of fear. I was suffering.

Fear kept my mouth shut. I didn't speak up when people made fun of Christians. I compromised my values in the ways that I thought, talked, and acted. There was certainly no praying for people in the back of the rescue. If the light of God was shining through me at all, it was very dim.

Eventually the day came in the Blazer, when God slapped me out of my stupor. Some of the first resources God brought to me were all about fear. God used different people to teach me what fear is and how to get rid of it. I was able to put some understanding behind 2 Timothy 1:7,

> For God hath not given us the spirit of fear; but of power, and of love, and of a sound mind.

I learned that fear is a spirit sent by Satan to destroy people. I also learned that fear is a sin. We are commanded not to fear 365 times in the Bible in different variations covering worry, dread, anxiety, and all other types of fear. God gently showed me that I needed to repent for living my life full of fear. I became aware that by living in fear, I was telling God He wasn't big enough to take care of me. I learned that after repentance comes deliverance. I told the spirit of fear to leave my life in Jesus' name, and I began to understand the authority I had been given over fear through Christ.

For a long time my spiritual life and work life had remained separate. As my journey with God progressed, I had the amazing revelation that I should begin to take God with me as I responded to emergency calls. As I began to extend myself to God, He began to extend Himself through me.

Step Into the Water

One morning the Lord led me to the book of Joshua:

Tell the priests who carry the Ark of the Covenant: "When you reach the edge of the Jordan's waters, go and stand in the river." ... And as soon as the priests who carry the ark of the LORD—the Lord of all the earth—set foot in the Jordan, its waters flowing downstream will be cut off and stand up in a heap. — Joshua 3:8, 13 (NIV)

As I read through the familiar story of how God dried up the Jordan so that His people could cross, I thought, "Pretty neat story, but I don't see anything new." As I closed the Bible, I thought about the instructions God gave Joshua. I wondered why God wanted the twelve chosen men to actually stand in the river with the heavy Ark before He would move on their behalf. God began to softly speak to my heart. We often stand on the "bank" looking over at our problems and issues saying, "Alright God, I need you to take care of this mess. I need you to perform this miracle and heal me or deliver me, but I am not going to get my feet wet. I am going to stand here where it's dry while you do the work. After all, there's nothing wrong with me. There couldn't possibly be anything I might need to do before you move on my behalf."

I've got to let you in on something. God's not going to let you have it that way. It wasn't the way he operated for the nation of Israel, and it's not the way He operates with us. God requires us to participate in resolving our issues and problems. It's only when we engage our wills, take up our heavy burdens, and "step into the river" that God will move on our behalf. "Stepping into the river" will look different for everyone, but one thing is clear—God will ask you to do it.

Is it scary and uncomfortable? Yes! We can understand how scary it is when we consider how dangerous the Jordan River was

in this story. We are told in Joshua that the Jordan was flooded
because it was the time of the harvest:

> And as they that bare the ark were come unto Jordan, and the
> feet of the priests that bare the ark were dipped in the brim of
> the water, (for Jordan overfloweth all his banks all the time of
> harvest. — Joshua 3:15

The Jordan was not only a treacherous river with many rapids
and currents, but it was also overflowing, which made it all the
more dangerous. It would have appeared, in the natural, foolish to
stand in it because of the danger of being swept away and killed.
The men were not only told to stand in the danger, but to also
carry the Ark with them. They had to stand in dangerous water
with a very heavy burden on their shoulders before God would
move on their behalf.

God not only asked for faith from Israel here, but also required
them to move in an act of obedience to demonstrate that faith.
James 2:17 tells us that faith without works is dead. It's one thing
to agree in our minds that God will move on our behalf. It's
another thing entirely to carry our heavy burdens into dangerous
water and trust that God will respond.

> What doth it profit, my brethren, though a man say he hath
> faith, and have not works? Can faith save him? — James 2:14

Our obedience testifies to our degree of faith, and it seems
that God often wants a demonstration of faith before He moves
for us. The Bible seems to paint a picture of a God whose top
priority is relationship—His with us and ours with Him. I believe
God passionately wants to deliver us from all things that make
us suffer. But I believe that an even greater passion of His is the
development of intimate relationship with us. That relationship is
tried, proven and developed through our obedience. Jesus said in
John 14:15, "If you love me keep my commands."

I wonder what would have happened if the twelve men would
not have carried that heavy Ark into the treacherous water. Would

God have said with much grief, "They're still not ready." Would He have made the nation wander longer in the wilderness? It is not God's desire for us to live forever in the wilderness. If you are stuck in the wilderness, then it may be time to evaluate the attitude of your heart. Does your heart desire the things that God's heart desires? Are you truly ready to submit to Him regardless of the cost?

In his book, *The Three Battlegrounds,* Francis Frangipane writes:

> While it is true that He (Jesus) is our promised land, it is also true that we are His promised land! The giants within our hearts, though they have withstood and humbled us, shall not withstand Him! He is the eternal Joshua, the Holy One who knows no defeat!

Have you carried your heavy burdens into the dangerous water, or are you standing on the bank where it's comfortable and controlled? I stood on the bank of the river for most of my life afraid of the rushing water. But then my life changed, and I was ready to jump in. I was ready to engage with God. I was ready for a relationship. In Romans 12:2 Paul says, "*And be not conformed to this world: but be ye transformed by the renewing of your mind, that ye may prove what is that good, and acceptable, and perfect, will of God.*" For me walking free from fear meant being transformed and having my mind renewed. My mind was made new as I practiced faith instead of fear. I was "washed by the water of the Word!"

Fear Defeated

I had the privilege of seeing fear defeated in my family one day as I was sitting beside my son Rylie on an airplane getting ready for a flight from Tampa to Kansas City. As we taxied down the runway, Rylie grasped my arm. He enjoyed flying, but he wasn't crazy about taking off and landing. Rylie was six at the time, so his response wasn't unexpected. But I thought it was a perfect opportunity to practice trust. Kara and I have taught our children about spiritual warfare and whom our fight is really against. Rylie has been given the knowledge and tools to defeat Satan and his attack of fear. I turned to him and gently said, "Tell fear to go." He looked at me, not relaxing his tight grip on my arm at all and said, "Fear go in the name of Jesus." Understanding that deliverance is only a part of the battle, I asked him, "Does your Daddy God love you?" He replied, "Yes." I asked him, "Do you trust Him to keep you and this plane safe?" He responded with a firm, "Yes." I then explained to him that Jesus is not only concerned with what we say, but He also watches how we live. I told Rylie that he needed to practice trusting. He looked at me and I said, "Trust Him." I moved his hand off of my arm and put his hand in mine. The plane sped down the runway, and I repeated, "Trust Him." Rylie had his eyes closed, but what I was saying was getting through and penetrating his soul. The plane lifted off the ground, and peace washed over my little boy. His whole body relaxed, and a smile crept over his face.

Thou wilt keep him in perfect peace, whose mind is stayed on thee: because he trusteth in thee. — Isaiah 26:3

From that point on, taking off and landing was no problem for Rylie. He didn't even want to hold my hand anymore. He was resting in peace because he trusted in his Father God. I learned a lesson from that. Times when I feel afraid, anxious, or stressed are just opportunities for me to practice trusting in God. If I trust, then I move closer to Jesus. If I stay in fear, I stall and can even move backward, allowing bondage back into my life. This applies not just to fear, but to unforgiveness as well. Offenses and injustices are difficult, but they are great opportunities to practice forgiveness. I know it's much easier said than done, but if we just "brush off" hurts, we will never move forward in forgiveness.

Submit yourselves therefore to God. Resist the devil, and he will flee from you. — James 4:7

Did you notice that this verse is action-based and is not a lesson in passivity? Most of us know this verse, but so many of us fail to apply it to our lives. As a result, Satan holds many Christians in captivity, as he did me for many years.

James is also giving us a lesson in humility. Verse six tells us that God resists the proud, but gives grace to the humble. These two verses work together to teach us how to be free. We must defeat pride before we can submit to God. It takes humility to defeat our adversary's influence on our lives.

Fear and Idolatry

What we fear is what we will serve. Whom we fear is whom we will serve. It can't be any other way. Whatever or whomever we fear holds the ultimate power over us. They become idols in our lives.

> Their sorrows shall be multiplied that hasten after another god. — Psalm 16:4

I feel this is an important word for us as we enter some of the most important days any of us have ever experienced. Many of us would say, "Of course we can expect bad things if we are chasing after other gods." But are we really aware of what the "other gods" are in our lives?

I have come to understand other gods as "idols." In other words, those things we fear the most. It takes some deep self-evaluation and honesty to determine what the idols in our lives are. Willfully doing that takes great courage and humility. Many times pride blinds us to what those idols are, so it's important to ask God to shout out our iniquities to us. David said, *"Search me, O God, and know my heart: try me, and know my thoughts: And see if there be any wicked way in me, and lead me in the way everlasting."* (Ps. 139:23, 24).

What do you fear? What do you trust in more than God? Is it your job, checking account, friends, family, material possessions, social status, church, pastor, or your health? If you trust in any or all of these things, they are the "other gods" you are hastening after, and you can expect your pain, negative circumstances, distress, and sickness to multiply. It doesn't matter how much you go to church, see the lost saved, spend time in devotions, provide for your family, serve others, pray, preach, give, fast, or succeed at work. If THE God is not YOUR ONLY God, then your sorrows are going to multiply.

It's time for the Bride of Christ to leave fear in the dust (Rev. 19:7-8). It's time to trample all over the snakes and scorpions and to move into everything God has for us (Luke 10:19). No longer will fear hold us back. There is a cry and a call coming out of Heaven to be courageous, and God's children are responding! The workers are going into the fields to set the captives free (Matt. 9:37-38). Fear not!

Questions For Thought:

- What are the things causing you stress, anxiety, worry, or dread? What are those "other gods" you have been serving?

- Are those things preventing you from moving forward on the journey God has and desires for you? In what ways?

- Is it your heart's desire to replace your fear with total trust in God? In what areas of your life is God asking you to release fear and control? (Ask Him!)

- In what ways do you feel like God is asking you to step into the water?

CHAPTER 5

SATAN, GET OUT OF MY RESCUE!

"When by the malice of enemies God's people are brought to greatest straits, there is deliverance near to be sent from God unto them." – David Dickson

It was a pretty busy day at work, and we were already well into the groove when we were called to a young man and woman lying on the floor screaming in pain. We received no further information. We arrived on the scene to find a boy and girl on the floor in the bathroom. The young lady was screaming hysterically without any obvious reason. The boy with her had no idea why she was screaming. As soon as I heard her screaming, I heard the Lord tell me that a demon was manifesting through the girl. There wasn't anything physically wrong with her. She wasn't acting like she was drunk or on drugs. She was able to answer all of my questions appropriately except when I asked her why she was screaming. She didn't answer that question.

We wrapped her in a blanket and picked her up off of the floor. We led her out of the house and toward our rescue. As we walked, I asked the Lord what was going on. I heard the Lord tell me that the girl had been sexually abused. As she was being intimate with her boyfriend prior to our arrival, her traumatic memories were triggered, and the demon began to manifest.

My partner and I loaded her into the rescue, and I prepared her for transport. My partner began to drive us to the hospital. I talked to her as the Holy Spirit led me. I told her that she needed to be honest with me and that she wasn't in trouble. After reassuring her of these things, I asked her if she had ever been sexually abused. Her eyes became wide and filled with intense pain as she said that she had been when she was little. My heart broke as I saw the grief on the girl's face. She had suffered under the weight of that great tragedy her whole life. I gently asked her if she wanted to be free from the torment she had experienced ever since that trauma. She looked at me with hope mixed with desperation, and through tears said, "Yes."

I led her in a prayer of dedicating and committing her life to the Lord. Next I led her in forgiving the person who had abused her. She took great courage and forgave that person. Then she began to repent of different things as the Lord showed her. She was being washed clean. Next I led her in binding her demonic tormentors and breaking the chains they had wrapped around her. She did all of this with a determination and authority that surprised me, coming from someone who just turned her life over to God.

In the name of Jesus I bound and cast out the demons that the Lord showed me were there. At the Lord's leading, I also prophesied the Lord's words to her and blessed her. The girl was transformed before my eyes. The screaming was gone. Her eyes had lost all hopelessness and despair. Death had lost its sting. Grief was replaced by joy. She was smiling a glowing smile. A blanket of peace covered the young lady as she encountered the Lord in a powerful way. Her face streamed with tears in wonder of a God who loved her enough to reach out to her in such a dramatic way. When I found her, she was screaming. When I left her, she couldn't stop smiling. When I found myself back at the hospital a few hours later I looked in on her, and the smile hadn't faded at all. That's the power of God! I am continually amazed and overwhelmed by the Almighty.

Enough!

Many people are very familiar with panic or anxiety attacks. I have responded to a ton of them over the years. The attacks can vary in severity. Sometimes they can be so severe, they will completely incapacitate the person, creating a need for sedation.

One day we were dispatched to a young man having a panic attack. We arrived to find him lying on the floor curled up in the fetal position, completely incapacitated. Normally this would be a sedation case. It probably takes at least fifteen minutes for a person having an average panic attack to begin to calm down; someone having an attack as severe as this man was often wouldn't calm down even after sedation. He was having a major episode. As I approached the man, I began to pray. I took authority over the spirit of fear, bound it, and told it to leave.

We picked the man up off of the floor and held him in a chair. I turned around to get something, and when I faced the patient again, his breathing had returned to normal, and he was acting appropriately. This was only a minute or two after I had commanded the spirit of fear to leave! The power of the enemy was broken as the power of God filled the room. It was enough to elicit some comments of wonder from my partner about how fast the patient was recovering. I had never seen someone recover that quickly. It was purely the power of God. I have found that when God is my partner, I often say, "I have never seen that before."

What Must I do?

It was a very warm afternoon when the tones went off, calling us to a person having irregular heartbeats. We arrived on the scene and were directed to a young man. We'll call Jim. He was breathing fast and looking distressed. I approached and asked him what was wrong. Jim explained that he had experienced some heart-related issues in the past and suffered from an occasional rapid heartbeat. He explained that he had seen many different doctors, none of whom had been able to explain why he was experiencing the issues he did.

We helped Jim to the rescue, and a short time later we were heading toward the hospital. We had only been on the road for a minute or so when Jim suddenly began to tell me about his life. He told me about some of the hard things he was going through. He shared fears and hopes along with pain and tragedy. I couldn't help but wonder why this guy was pouring his heart out to me. I hadn't asked him about his life. My heart was pricked with emotion as I realized what happens when the light of God shines through us. It draws people searching for hope and purpose.

I listened to Jim talk. His words were saturated with despair. When he finished I told him softly that it sounded like he was trying to figure out how to get some peace in his life. His eyes lit up as he urgently told me that I was exactly right. All he wanted was some peace. We rode together in a moment of silence as I silently asked the Lord to show me how to respond. I asked the Lord for the next steps to take in order to make the peace he wanted a reality. But Jim broke the silence by asking me the best question anyone could ever ask. "What do I have to do to be free?" My heart skipped a beat. I was blown away; did Jim just ask me to tell him how he could be free? Did I just hear correctly? I had to take a moment to gather myself. Could there be any better lead into sharing the power of the gospel? With a mix of joy and shock on my face I asked, "How is your relationship with Jesus?" Jim told me that he didn't have one. Over the next ten minutes or so, I eagerly shared the gospel with Jim. We walked through repentance for sin and forgiveness for those who had hurt him. Jim forgave himself for the way he was living his life and committed his life to God. Together we bound and broke the power of the enemy in his life, and he was delivered from the chains that had held him prisoner and captive to sin. I watched as God restored Jim's identity as a chosen and called son of God and unleashed a tidal wave of peace into his soul. It was the peace Jim so desperately wanted, but up until that time had been missing. Jim didn't have any physical problems with his heart while we were together. A smile glowed radiantly on his face. When I left Jim at the hospital, he was a totally different person than when I first met him.

Over the years I have experienced many people who I had just met begin to pour their hearts out to me. I can't explain this other than to say that when you are being transformed by God, you become a light in the darkness, and people are drawn to you. It's an amazing thing when people come to you asking for Jesus.

Let God Heal Your Grief

It was our first call of the day, and it was for a woman who had reportedly fainted. When we arrived on the scene, we found a woman lying on the floor. She was able to answer all of my questions. She told us that she felt fine other than some weakness. She said that she felt like she might faint again. She explained that occasional fainting had been going on for about a year. My partner and I helped her up off of the floor and onto the stretcher. We took her out to the rescue and prepared her for transport.

We were less than a mile down the road when I felt the Holy Spirit stir inside of me. He told me to ask the woman some specific questions. Her answers revealed pain and trauma. In the last two years, she had lost her husband and her son. I was overcome by sorrow and compassion for this woman. The Lord spoke to my heart and told me that the woman had a relationship with Him. I gently asked her about her experience with God. She told me that she talked to Him a lot and that she had a good relationship with Him. It was then that the Lord spoke to me the word "grief"— that He wanted to heal her broken heart and take away all of the grief. I told her what God was showing me, and she nodded in agreement. But there was a block somewhere in her heart. There was an emotional hindrance and demonic stronghold denying access to that grief and pain. One principle I know to be true is that to heal from trauma, we have to be able to access the traumatic emotions. I didn't know what to do next, so I looked at her and asked her if I could pray for her. She said yes. When in doubt, pray!

I began to pray over the woman the words God was speaking to my heart. I could feel the presence of God fill the rescue, but when I looked at her, God showed me that His glory wasn't getting past the emotional wall she had allowed to surround her heart. The wall was her attempt to keep the pain out. It was discouraging. I knew God was with us, and I knew that he wanted to do something amazing for the woman. I continued to pray over her as the Lord led, and I began to engage in spiritual warfare on her behalf. The Lord gave me some prophetic words to encourage her and plant hope, but there was still no response from her. It was as if an invisible shield around her was deflecting God's arrows. I was frustrated and asked God what I should do next.

God answered and told me to verbally release His Spirit of Peace over her. So I did. The moment I audibly released the Spirit of Peace over her in the name of Jesus, something happened. It was as if a gale-force wind rushed through the rescue and compelled the woman to breathe it in. She took it in with three dramatic gasps. It looked as if she was inflated. The look on her face was one of shock and bewilderment. Then her face changed again to reflect perfect peace! Her countenance changed along with the atmosphere. The block had been removed from her heart. She had been set free.

We pulled into the hospital. I found out a little later that bad traffic had delayed the usual time it takes to get to the hospital—enough time for God to do what He wanted to do in the woman's heart. It was only because of my extended time with her that we were able to get to freedom. God knew what He was doing and fixed the traffic to give us the time.

God had another prophetic word and a promise for this woman, and they were the last things I said to her. I believe that what I told her is a word and promise from God for anyone who has had to deal with terrible trauma and grief. The word is this: "Stop waiting to die, and begin to speak life!" The promise is this: "As you allow me to heal your pain and take away your grief, I will bring healing and restoration to your body."

We should pay close attention to the first part of that promise. We are the ones who have to face pain. We are the ones who have to stop burying hurt and wounds. We are the ones who have to allow ourselves to "feel." We are the ones who need to allow God to heal us. It's a promise that requires something from us. Don't be afraid! God is with you.

CHAPTER 6

SEPARATED

Jesus said unto him, 'Thou shalt love the Lord thy God with all thy heart, and with all thy soul, and with all thy mind. This is the first and great commandment. And the second is like unto it, Thou shalt love thy neighbor as thyself. On these two commandments hang all the law and the prophets.' — Matthew 22:37-40

On April 8, 1982, a little boy pushed his way into the world. That little boy was named Jesse Michael Birkey. He emerged looking for something he could recognize. He emerged desperate to grab onto something solid. In those beginning moments outside of the womb, Jesse searched and pleaded for something with his little infant spirit and soul. He was searching for love. Not love as many of us understand love to be—emotional, unstable, and failing—but a rock-solid foundation of love to sustain him, a love to bring comfort security and acceptance to his world.

I tell you the truth, no one can see the kingdom of God unless he is born again. — John 3:3 (NIV)

Jesus says here that everyone who wants to enter the kingdom of God must be born again. For that to be true, it means that no one is born into the kingdom of God the first time around. That means that every single person on this earth is in need of a Savior.

King David said in Psalm 51:5, "Surely I was sinful at birth, sinful from the time my mother conceived me." I believe that David is trying to give us some insight here into our hopelessness from birth and into every single person's need for salvation. Sin separates us from God and is, in reality, death (Isa. 59:2; Rom. 6:23). David states that he was born sinful and thus separated from God. A devastating consequence of this is that to be separated from God is to be separated from love. God is love (1 John 4:8).

Paul states that before we come to Jesus we are dead in our trespasses (Eph. 2:1). This is a physical metaphor, but a spiritual reality. This is the death that passed down through generations because of Adam and Eve's original sin. If Adam and Eve hadn't sinned in the Garden of Eden, then David would have been born into eternal life—that is, if nobody else had sinned before him.

It's the same for us as it was for David. When we are born, we are separated from God. That might be hard to swallow. But to say it any other way would mean that not everyone would need to be "born again" prior to entering the kingdom of God or that there is a point between birth and the age of accountability at which God severs our connection with Him and we have to choose to get it back. Neither of those options makes sense to me, though I absolutely believe that children who die prior to the age of accountability go to be with God. I attribute this to His great love and mercy. From the moment we are conceived, we are desperate for salvation.

Babies and children up to a certain age lack the ability to choose between right and wrong, for God or against Him. Because of this they lack the ability to make a choice for salvation. As long as they lack that ability, they remain separated from God and love. But God has a plan for this dilemma. Those who love God are referred to as His children (1 John 3:2). This shows a parent-child relationship. In the absence of our ability to choose God as our father, God established a human parent-child system with the purpose being to show that child who God is and to reflect God's nature to the child. This is a heavy charge to parents! We are instructed to show our children the nature of God, teach them His desires, teach them about salvation, teach them His ways, and above all reflect to them the perfect love of God so that when they *can* choose God, they *will* choose Him (Eph. 6:1-4; Prov. 22:6, 23:13-14; Deut. 6:4-9, 4:9-10, 11:19; 2 Cor. 12:13-15; 1 Tim. 5:3-4; Joel 1:2-3; Ps. 78:2-8, 103:13).

The problem is that the recurring theme throughout history seems to be that God makes a plan, and we mess it up. The unfortunate truth is that all have sinned and fall short of God's glory (Rom. 3:23). Those who love God are *being* perfected and *being* conformed to the image of Christ, but none of us here on earth have arrived yet (Col. 1:28; Rom. 8:29). That means that we all are in various stages of imperfection when we have our children. Those of us who love God will pass on a mixture of blessings and curses to our children. Because of the areas of our hearts that we have allowed God to heal, we will be able to pass on generational blessings to our children and instruct them in the ways of God (Deut. 7:9). Because of the areas of our hearts that haven't been healed, we will pass on generational curses to our children and teach them the ways of the world. Generational sin is biblical, and it's found in the following passages:

> Thou shalt not bow down thyself to them, nor serve them: for I the LORD thy God am a jealous God, visiting the iniquity of the fathers upon the children unto the third and fourth generation of them that hate me. — Exodus 20:5

> The LORD is longsuffering, and of great mercy, forgiving iniquity and transgression, and by no means clearing the guilty, visiting the iniquity of the fathers upon the children unto the third and fourth generation. — Numbers 14:18

> Thou shalt not bow down thyself unto them, nor serve them: for I the LORD thy God am a jealous God, visiting the iniquity of the fathers upon the children unto the third and fourth generation of them that hate me. — Deuteronomy 5:9

The sobering fact in this is that all of our children are/were at the mercy of our ability as parents to adhere to God's parental charge. Our ability to adhere to God's charge is directly related to our degree of transformation. The more transformed and healed we are, the more we are able to reflect God to our children. The more we reflect God to our children, the less room there is for our adversary to establish himself in their hearts. The less we reflect God to our children, the more room there is for our adversary to establish himself in their hearts.

My Struggle to Find Love

In my early years I experienced a mixture of incredible blessings but also fell victim to some generational curses and unhealed areas of my parents' hearts. Some of the generational curses that affected me very early on were rejection, worthlessness, and insecurity. As I grew, I chose to believe the lies Satan told me about my value and worth. My foundation was not built on the limitless and unfathomable love of God. Instead it was built on feelings of rejection, worthlessness, and insecurity. Feeling that I was a failure and unlovable was woven into my identity. My disconnection from the love of God was the reason I lived in so much fear.

> There is no fear in love; but perfect love casteth out fear: because fear hath torment. He that feareth is not made perfect in love. — 1 John 4:18

Because the perfect love of God was not a part of my foundation, I had nothing with which to drive fear out of my life. God wanted to teach me about His love, but I ignored Him. I chose to stay in rejection, worthlessness, and insecurity. I chose to remain outside of love. I rejected the one who loved me more than I could ever imagine, and as result was locked even further in the chains of the enemy. I believed the lies Satan told me about being unworthy of God.

God has given us all the desire, no, the desperation to be loved. So what happens when we are separated from it? We search for it desperately. If we have chosen to reject the love of God, then we will be desperate to fill our "love tank" wherever we can. As I grew through elementary school, I tried to fill my love tank from friends. This made being chosen for games at school, being invited to birthday parties, and all other group activities very important in my life. My self-worth rode on these things.

Looking back, it was strange how being chosen for those things never built up any buffer against the rare occasion when I was not chosen. Not being chosen would wreck me. It just reinforced what I already believed about myself being unworthy and unlovable. When our identity is not woven into the perfect love of God, we ride an emotional roller coaster controlled by other people's actions.

As I progressed through middle school and the first year of high school, I added girls and sports to try meet my love need. Nothing was able to sustain me at all. Being picked on during this time kept me pretty low. Changing high schools put an end to the bullying, but the damage was done.

Then I got involved with pornography. It was another attempt to make myself feel good. As we progress through life bound in chains, our enemy will move us toward things that only further entrench us in his grasp. Pornography added guilt, shame, and condemnation to my life. There were times that I felt the only way out of the torment was death. The enemy was using me as a punching bag as I continued to reject the one who loved me more than I could ever imagine. But I was angry that God wouldn't deliver me from my afflictions and bondage. I wanted God to deliver me, but I was living in rebellion.

Even in the midst of my rebellion God, by His great love, decided to pour out some blessings into my life. In one year, I got married and started my career as a firefighter/paramedic. I added my wife and work to my list of love-tank fillers. Now I was looking to get my tank filled by friends, sports, pornography, work, and my wife. And as if that wasn't enough, I eventually added gambling to the mix.

Addictions are interesting things—terrible but interesting. The addiction is not actually to the substance or act, but to the release of dopamine causing a feeling of euphoria to course through the body. Dopamine is naturally produced in all of our bodies. In sex and pornography, the release happens at orgasm. The release in gambling comes the moment just before you find out if you win or lose. Recreational drugs cause a dopamine release as well. It's the same with alcohol. Food can also release dopamine. Are you getting the picture? What we really become addicted to is the euphoria we get, which we associate with love. At the root of all addictions is the desperation to be loved. It isn't very hard to understand why people become addicted and why the only way to be free is to be filled, renewed, and transformed by the perfect love of God. Addictions of any kind show us that there are still walls around our hearts blocking the only love that can set us free, God's love.

Work became a part of my identity. I allowed it to define me. Firefighters are generally well liked and respected. I allowed myself to be built up by that. I was driven and strived to become the best firefighter/paramedic in the department. God blessed me with the skill set to be a very capable paramedic, and I received a lot of recognition for my performance, which I allowed to validate me. There is a huge problem with that. The problem is that nobody is perfect, and mistakes will be made. It didn't matter how much attention I received for doing a good job. The times I learned by making mistakes pulverized my soul. Just one mistake was enough to make me question my value, not just as a firefighter/paramedic, but also as a person. Mistakes would send me into a downward spiral, and I would be down for days. I would have to work very hard at picking myself up, and since there was a separation from love, the issues were never really dealt with. I would just strive harder to be better the next time. I found this to be an exhausting way to live. All of the validation received from my good work seemed to pass very quickly, leaving me empty again. Is this cycle familiar to you?

Because soaking in the affections of others means not offending them, my spiritual influence at work was pretty much non-existent. The light of God was distant in me because I wouldn't let Him in. I was so much more concerned with fitting in rather than being set apart. Fitting in was where my acceptance and self-worth came from. The stronghold of the "unloving" (self-hatred, self-rejection, self-resentment, self-unforgiveness, shame, guilt, condemnation) was maybe the largest block to my ability to share Jesus with my co-workers and patients. I didn't share Jesus with anyone.

I was merely just surviving in life. I was wrecked by guilt, shame, condemnation, feelings of inadequacy, and so much more. I didn't feel like I was worthy of anything good in my life. Everything in my life was affected by my separation from love. When my son was born, I loved him with all that I understood about love, but you can see how messed up my understanding was. I wasn't able to pour the perfect love of God into my son, and he was a very fearful child for the first four years of his life. In those years he was exposed to all of the bondage that held me captive spiritually. Rejection and insecurity latched onto him, and he was timid and had very little confidence. My daughter was born, and it was the same story for her in the first eighteen months of her life.

My marriage was mostly superficial. There wasn't much depth to anything in my life. I wouldn't let people get close because if I didn't like myself then why would anyone else like me? That was a question I didn't want to answer.

I couldn't go on the way that I was. I began to recognize that the only answer out there for me was God. I began to realize that I didn't really know Him at all. All I had was head knowledge. True revelation was absent in my life. I had built my foundation on sand, and it was crumbling beneath my feet.

Finally Connected

Looking back I realize that there was an intense battle being fought for my soul during that season in my life. God was desperately trying to get my attention, but it was still my choice to respond to Him. My Blazer experience couldn't have come at a more crucial time. It was then that I made the choice to be transformed by God, and He resurrected my spirit and soul. The dormant parts of me sprung to life, and I began to live for what felt like the very first time. It was like going from black and white to a world full of intense and beautiful colors.

In the months that followed, God began to awaken my suppressed emotions and I began to "feel" again. It was during that time God called me to my forty-day fast. Not everyone needs to fast for forty days to be in obedience. Fasting is not the key to seeing God move; obedience is the key. But for me it was during that fast that God brought the largest breakthrough regarding the "unloving" bondage in my life. Freedom came shortly after I listened to a teaching on the bondage of the "unloving" and how it manifests in our lives. I quickly realized I was manifesting the "unloving" bondage, and I wanted it gone as quickly as possible.

Repentance was and is the critical first step, and I repented for believing the enemy's lies about my worth. I also repented for rejecting the love of God. I repented for trying to get my love from so many other sources. I then told God that I received His forgiveness. I believe it's important to speak out loud that we receive God's forgiveness. There is power in our spoken words (Prov. 18:21).

The next step was to command every spirit that was telling me I was worthless and unlovable to leave. I commanded all of the lying spirits to leave along with all shame, guilt, and condemnation. I also told all spirits of self-hatred and bitterness to leave. I still remember the freedom I felt as the tormentors left me. It was then that I began asking for new revelations of God's love for me. I began to plead with God to pour His perfect love all over me. Suddenly I was overcome with God's love in a way that I had never experienced. It drove me to my knees and then onto my face. I could feel the weight of it on me. It saturated my entire being. I was filled with such emotion that the tears flowed freely. It was incredible. The joy and peace was amazing. I said, "God, I want more! Give me more! I want it all!"

God spoke, and I clearly remember him gently saying, *"Jesse, if I were to pour out all of My love on you it would kill you."* God is love. God was pouring out himself onto me. We as humans can only handle so much. God was giving me all that I could handle. When the apostle Paul wrote about the love of God that surpasses all knowledge, he was not just making a cute little analogy. Paul was really saying that we truly cannot understand or comprehend the full love of God. To know love is to know God. We as humans can get a glimpse, but we cannot comprehend it all.

As God's love poured into me, I was finally able to find the strength to forgive myself for all the things I was still holding myself in condemnation for. It was as if my soul could finally breathe as the chains of self-blame, guilt, and condemnation were obliterated.

That was an amazing experience, and from that point on things began to change in me. Suddenly the scripture I had read about who I am in Christ and what God thinks about me came to life. The Bible started to speak directly to my soul. I began to change the way I related to my wife. I was complete, honest, and open. I was not afraid of being vulnerable anymore. I was done protecting myself. I started to talk about feelings and started to truly love Kara. I was finally beginning to have the relationship with God I had always wanted and the type of marriage that I always wanted. I found I actually wanted to spend lots of time with Kara. I just wanted to be with her. I found that I wanted to share my day with her, and when she would ask me questions, I wanted to answer them and didn't feel like she was intruding.

I began to experience love for my kids that was independent of my own need for love. I was showing them God's love instead of "love" that hoped to get acceptance and validation in return. They responded by forming a solid foundation in the perfect love of God. I watched as fear left my son and he began to show leadership qualities instead of following others. He was finding security in the love of God that I was finally able to reflect to him. He was being transformed. My daughter was responding in the same way.

I took this new-found freedom to work with me, and it was then that God started to build testimonies. I was finally willing to be used. The light of God began to shine through me because His love was and is strong! People began to notice and made comments that I wasn't the same as I used to be.

It was only when I was able to receive love that God was able to use me to pour love into others. That's true for all of us. We can't give something we don't have. If you have the love of God, people will know. If you have it, the fruit of your life will testify to it. I was bearing good fruit for what felt like the first time in my life.

A couple of months after my amazing experience with God's love, I was spending some time with God by myself, and I had a vision. I saw a man on a beach. Every so often a large wave would come and crash over the man, and then the water would recede. Even though the water had receded, the sand that the man was standing on was still wet. The Lord spoke and said, *"This is what My love is like free from bondage. There are specific times when I pour out My love onto My people in power, and it leaves them totally drenched (the waves). That feeling does not last forever. It recedes. However, their souls (sand) are still wet with the knowledge of My love, and it never dries out."* When we walk in God's love free from bondage, we walk with the constant knowledge and understanding of His love for us. That does not mean that we will always feel the power of it, but what it does mean is that we will never forget it.

> And so we know and rely on the love God has for us. God is love. Whoever lives in love lives in God, and God in him. — 1 John 4:16 (NIV)

We experience the love of God, but we also rely on it in the wilderness times when we don't necessarily feel it.

God set me free, but that doesn't mean there weren't times of testing the new-found freedom. My wife's confession of infidelity came after my journey of transformation began and shook my whole world. My first book, *Marriage: What's The Point*, tells the story of that season of trauma, pain, and miraculous restoration. But the love of God held us together as He put back together again what was broken.

Greg Boyd writes in *The Myth of a Christian Nation*:

> As we learn to think, feel, and act under God's rule, we learn how to get our worth, significance, and security from

Christ alone. We learn how to be freed from our addiction to futilely trying to acquire worth, significance, and security for ourselves. We learn how to walk in freedom from violence, self-centeredness, materialism, nationalism, racism, and all other false ways of getting life. As we die to our old self and "put on" our "new self" created in Christ Jesus (Ephesians 4:22-24), we learn how to be loved and how to love God, ourselves, our neighbor, our enemies, as well as the animal kingdom and the earth God originally placed under our dominion and loving care (Genesis 1:28-30).

The Problem of Self Unforgiveness

One of the most important and critical steps of my "learning how to be loved" was making the choice to truly forgive myself. I was only able to do this after understanding that Satan was the one lying to me about my worth and value my whole life. When I finally began to believe the truth about my value and worth according to God, the walls came down, and I was able to forgive myself. I was set free from a lifetime of guilt and shame.

Many times ministry with individuals will be going great until we come to self-forgiveness. I often hear, "I just can't forgive myself." But the importance of self-forgiveness can't be ignored, and the benefits are amazing! One of my best friends (and mentor) Richard Mull shares this testimony in his book, *Lord Heal Me.*

One woman came to us with a severe form of arthritis that had begun to attack her extremities. Her fingers were turning black and needed to be amputated. A family member had brought her to us after reading my book, *The Jesus Training Manual.* I researched the spiritual roots of this form of arthritis and found it to be extreme self-hatred. This was new to me, and I didn't even fully trust the information that I had at the time, but I was open to testing it.

When I met the woman, her hands were completely bandaged, and she was scheduled to have her fingers amputated later that same week. In a quest to determine the root of any possible self-hatred, I was led by God to ask her if there was anything in her life for which she could never forgive herself. At this point she began to cry and asked if her daughter would leave. Then she opened up about some things that had taken place when she was younger that caused her great shame. One of the issues was an abortion she had many, many years ago. Her tears really flowed, and for the next little while we grieved together over what had taken place both to her and as a result of her own choices. She asked for the Lord's forgiveness and worked toward receiving God's forgiveness and forgiving herself. This was very hard for her.

Do you see how what was troubling her spirit was also troubling her joints, bones, and extremities? Years of guilt, self-hatred, self-rejection, and torment had taken its toll on her body. Satan is known as the accuser of the brother (Rev. 12:10), and this woman had been tormented throughout her life by spirits that reminded her of her sin, questioned how God could forgive someone for what she had done, and taught her to hate herself. She was not always aware of these thoughts or how they affected her. Throughout her life, many instances reinforced this self-rejection and self-hatred. Her body had taken all of the rejection it could handle and was now falling apart. But God broke through, set her free emotionally, healed her wounded spirit, set her soul free from the captivity to past sins, and touched her body with the healing power of the Holy Spirit.

The healing manifested first in her countenance. This woman looked twenty years younger. The weight of the sins that had been crushing her was lifted that night. Later that same week when it came time to amputate her fingers, the doctors removed her bandages and found her fingers to be completely normal and healthy!

God has been so faithful to me when it comes to love. I have been saturated with love since my day of freedom. Addictions are no longer in my life. God delivered me from addictions as He poured His sustaining love into me. He wants to pour His sustaining love into you too! See the lies for what they are and allow God to knock down the walls around your heart with His truth. There is no greater love than that of the Lover for His beloved (John 15:11)!

Questions For Thought

- In what ways did your parents struggle to show you the perfect love of God?

- What events in your life formed your negative perception of yourself (personal choices, being victimized through abuse or other tragedies)?

- What lies has our adversary told you about your value and self-worth?

- What does God say about you regarding your value and self-worth?

- Forgiving yourself can be very difficult. In what ways do you see a need for self- forgiveness in your life? Are you ready to take that step and cover your past sins in the blood of Jesus? (Ask God for help!)

CHAPTER 7

THE POWER OF GOD IS WITH YOU

"The kingdom of God does not consist in talk, but in power, that is, in works and practice. God loves the 'doers of the word' in faith and love, and not the 'mere hearers,' who, like parrots, have learned to utter certain expressions with readiness."
– Martin Luther

Many of the experiences I have had with the power of God have happened outside of the fire department. Sometimes we think that we have to be in a certain job, ministry, or atmosphere to see God move in power. That is a lie! God wants to use us anytime, anywhere. Just say yes!

I am including testimonies of other regular, everyday people in the pages ahead. They are people without big ministries, titles, or positions. They are ordinary people who said, "Yes, Lord." That's all it takes.

An Unexpected Encounter

It was a very nice night, and I was headed to meet a friend of mine. I decided to go the back way to my friend's house because it runs by a Starbucks, and I wanted something to drink.

On the way out of my neighborhood I realized that I was ten miles or so over having an empty gas tank. The gas gauge on the car was broken, so we tracked our remaining gas based on how many miles we had driven. I started to pray that God would help me get to a gas station. A few minutes later my car began to sputter a little, and then it gave up completely.

I coasted for a block or so and came to a stop. There was a gas station just over the median. I thanked God as I crossed the street and pumped gas into my five-gallon gas can. I put enough gas in to get me across the street, and a short time later I was pumping gas into my car from the pump.

As I was filling up I happened to look up and there, sitting on the gas pump, was somebody's wallet. I picked it up and looked at it closely. There was plenty of cash inside and just about everything they tell you never to carry in your wallet. I knew that whoever left it there was going crazy looking for it. I finished filling my tank, and checked inside the store in case anyone had stopped by asking about it. The attendant told me nobody had asked, and he didn't recognize the photo on the ID.

I started to understand that God was orchestrating the whole night. I sensed that He wanted me to go get my friend before I took the wallet to its owner, so I drove to my friend's house. My friend was less than enthusiastic about returning someone's wallet so late at night, but I was finally able to drag him out of the house. We looked up the wallet owner's address, and soon we were slowly making our way down the owner's street.

When we arrived at the correct address, the owner (we'll call him Frank) was standing in the driveway, pacing. My friend and I got out of the car and approached Frank holding out his wallet. Frank was overcome with relief and told us how he had been back to that gas station looking for it. Frank said that he didn't have much hope that he would ever see it again. I looked at Frank and began to explain to him how God had orchestrated the whole event. I told him how I took a route I don't normally take to get to my friend's house and how I ran out of gas right next to the gas station where he left his wallet. I told Frank that God had worked the entire night out just to let him know that God still cared about him and was protecting him.

Frank was overcome with the revelation and, filled with emotion, he began to tell us how things were going poorly in his life. There were hardships in his work, marriage, and relationships, and he was blaming himself for everything. He was also dealing with health issues. (On a side note, do you want to know when God is pushing you to minister to someone? A big indicator is when strangers begin to pour out their hearts out to you!).

Standing before us was a broken man; a stranger to us, but a precious child to God. God began to speak to my heart, giving me words He wanted Frank to hear. We asked Frank if we could pray for him, and what followed was amazing. There was healing ministry, prophetic words, repentance, and deliverance all in Frank's driveway. The Holy Spirit began to give us insight into the things Frank was struggling with and the chains that were holding him. Frank's eyes were wide open as two complete strangers were telling him about things that were intimate to his heart.

As we ministered according to the Holy Spirit's leading, we saw a broken man being put back together as hope and perfect love from the Father found a resting place deep within him. He was visibly shaken by what God was doing inside of him. A peace washed over him, and he told us with a smile how long it had been since he had felt any peace. We talked with Frank for a few more minutes and then left. What an awesome night!

I encourage all of you to be willing vessels for God and ask Him to use you. If you ask Him, He will give you opportunities.

Someone Should Prophesy

Some of the most amazing ministry experiences I have had have been completely spontaneous. This is a testimony of how powerful God is when He completely surprises us. Kara and I had decided to go to an outdoor concert where a Christian music artist was performing. We gathered up the kids and left the house. It was a hot day that had only slightly cooled by the time the concert was starting, but we didn't mind since we were looking forward to the performance.

The concert began with worship. The singer was engaged in something called "prophetic worship" in which a band plays music and the singer sings words God gives him/her to sing. It's not planned or written beforehand. As this was happening, the spiritual atmosphere began to change, and the Holy Spirit began to move across the field. My spirit was stirred, and I told God, "It would be great if someone began to prophetically minster." God answered and said, "You're right! Go ahead."

I was slightly taken back at the response because I did not feel prepared to minister to anyone. I tentatively said "Oh—okay, Lord. To whom?" The Lord showed me who He wanted to speak to, and I willed my feet to move toward the unsuspecting target. I grabbed Kara since we often minister as a team, and we slowly approached the man. When we reached him, I asked him if it would be OK if I shared with him a word from the Lord. He said it was okay. The words God spoke to this man through me were awesome in encouragement and edification. The Lord spoke acceptance and assurance to him, and he really needed it. We told the man everything the Lord gave us for him, and we started walking back toward our spot. I was thinking about how I was going to enjoy the concert when the Lord said, "You're not finished."

Kara and I ended up ministering to about ten different people during the concert, all complete strangers. People were amazed as the Lord spoke into their lives through us regarding specific issues and questions they were asking. Hearts were opened as God touched them and healed them. Many of them had never had experience with anything prophetic before, so they just stood there being blessed, their mouths hanging open in amazement. We saw so many things that day including tears, reconciliation, hope, joy, peace and freedom. We even made lifelong friends.

If you are willing, God will use you in places you never thought you would be used. The results will bless your heart and others.

A Full Tank

One night after a long day, I was on my way home with only one more stop to make. I was running low on fuel, so I had to stop at the gas station. I pulled in and noticed that there were only a few other vehicles filling up. I didn't find that out of the ordinary because it was pretty late. I pulled up next to the pump and opened my door when I began to hear God saying, *"I have an assignment for you."* I began to feel my spirit stir as I looked around to my right and saw a man who looked like he was in his thirties filling up with gas. The Lord said, *"I have a word for him."* I said, "Okay," and I approached the man. I reached him as he was finishing, and I introduced myself. I told him that the Lord had a word for him. He said, "Okay," with a skeptical look in his eyes. I began to speak the words God gave me for him, and his expression began to soften. His eyes filled with wonder and emotion. When I was finished speaking what God wanted me to speak, the man shook my hand and said, "Thank you so much. I really needed to hear that. You're exactly right in everything you said." The Lord had told me that the man had just lost his job and was facing a lot of financial hardships. The Lord wanted the man to know that if he kept his eyes on God, then everything would be fine. The Lord wanted the man to trust Him. The stranger filling up his gas tank was filled with despair, but he left that gas station filled with hope and peace. That's the power of God!

Loss Brings Life: Paige (mother, teacher)

About four years after we lost our baby through miscarriage, God used our traumatic event to help out a stranger in need. My friend and I were going to meet at my house for dinner. My friend told me that she wanted to bring one of her close friends with her. I didn't know the other person very well and had never spent any significant time with her.

That night, to my surprise, it ended up being just me and this other person because my friend couldn't make it. We began to talk, and I discovered that she had recently lost a pregnancy. It was not her first loss, and she did not have any children.

That night I shared with her about my loss and how God healed my pain and ministered into my brokenness. I knew God had brought me closer to Him through the pain, and I shared that with her. I told her that I felt God would use me through that tragedy. She told me God was using me to speak to her. She said she was always uncomfortable talking about God, but for some reason she wasn't uncomfortable talking about Him with me.

We were both in tears, and I told her that if the purpose of my tragedy was to be able to minister God's love to her, then it was worth it. To see her soften to God and start to be captured by love was worth the sadness I had experienced. We had a great conversation about God and how He blesses us when we seek His will for our life. We also talked about how He wants to give us the desires of our hearts. She didn't realize it that night, but found out later in the week that she was already pregnant again.

The Dream: Dawn (mother, housewife)

One morning I woke up and knew that God had given me a dream about a friend. I hadn't seen this particular friend in twelve years. God showed me in this dream that my friend, who is very musically talented, was writing a musical. Not a musical that you would see in a church, but one that you would see on a bigger scale.

In my dream God told me that I needed to tell my friend that if he would seek God with all his heart, the musical would be given to him. I went through my day wrestling with whether or not I should say something. I thought that maybe I should just leave it alone. God quickly reminded me that all He wants from us is obedience. I knew then and there that I was going to talk to my friend. I was a little nervous because I didn't know how he would accept what I had to tell him. Again God told me that it was not my responsibility how my friend accepted the message. It was only my responsibility to give the message. So I logged onto the computer and sent my friend the message God told me to give him.

A day later I received a message from my friend. He told me that he needed that message and thanked me for it. It made my heart joyful knowing that I had done the right thing and obeyed God.

Are You a Believer? Chuck (father, police officer)

I was frustrated. I was frustrated with the criminal justice system, frustrated with a society that increasingly calls for help (especially with parenting their kids), and frustrated with religion. As I was thinking about this and dealing with the emotions I was feeling, I noted that the radio was extra busy. The dispatchers were holding calls and asking anyone available to take them. Normally I would have jumped on some of them (suspicious persons and vehicles, aggressive drivers), but I was too burnt out and disgruntled to care. I was trying to ignore them and let a zone car or a new guy handle the nonsense for a while.

After ten more minutes of stewing and driving around looking for a traffic violation, I decided to check holding calls. One in particular caught my eye. It was a well-being check. A woman from out of state had called and asked us to check on her sister regarding suicidal thoughts and strange actions. Since she was calling from out of state, nothing was confirmed. It was all just hearsay. I hated those kinds of calls, but I took it. Luckily I was close by. I thought, *"Let me hurry up and check on this gal so I can get back to sulking in my frustration."* I walked up to the plain white door. There was a small sign that said, "As for me and my house, we will serve the Lord." I laughed inside at the absurdity and knocked on the door. I heard movement inside. After a minute, I knocked again. Still no one answered. I put my hand on my gun and thought through some scenarios in my mind. I knocked again, this time more forcefully. I heard a small voice say through the door, "Who is it?" I answered officially and identified myself as law enforcement. The voice answered, "What do you want?"

I recognized the voice to be female. It was an older voice and sounded slightly hoarse and tired. I said with authority, "Open the door and talk to me. I need to make sure you're alright." She hesitated. I used my flashlight to light up my front so she could

87

see my uniform through the peephole. She told me that she was in a wheelchair and she couldn't look through the peephole. She opened the door just a crack. She asked me again why I was there. I began to explain about the call from her sister and that we were making sure she was okay. The door opened another millimeter, but that was it. She explained that she was evicted recently from her apartment and didn't trust cops.

She said that she was fine and that her family had mistaken what she said. She said that she was trying to move and no one would help her and she had made some comments about dying, but only in frustration. She said she wasn't planning on hurting herself. Professionally, I was done; she was alive. She didn't say anything that I could use to take her to jail, and she appeared to be okay. I started to turn and say, "Have a nice day," when I remembered the sign. I asked her whose sign it was. She responded that it was her brother's house and he put it there, but that she was a believer.

She asked me if I was a believer. I told her I was. Everything changed. As soon as I finished saying the words, she flung open the door and motioned aggressively for me to come inside. Now that I could see her in the light, she reminded me of Jane Goodall. She was in a wheelchair, but her body seemed to lift up out of it. She began to tell me that she had spent all day praying for God to send her an answer. She wanted God to send her a messenger, to send her a "word." I started to realize that this was no accident. As she continued to hurriedly show me notes that she had been keeping about her prayers and the things she was asking God about, I prayed in my spirit for forgiveness. I had judged the woman. I had been rebellious and bitter the whole night. I asked God not only for forgiveness, but to fill me with His Spirit so that I might give her the "word" He had.

I asked the women if I could pray with her, and she excitedly said yes. We prayed, and God filled us. I felt joy, peace, patience, and love. I was blessed and in awe of a God who loved me so much that even though I was backbiting minutes before, He was still willing to use me to tell His daughter that He heard her cries and He loved her.

We talked for another ten minutes about the enemy and what he was doing in her home. Some of it involved a teenage girl, her niece. God gave me a vision about the girl. I saw her being held by the enemy, and he was using chains of drugs and sex to bind her. I also saw depression and a spirit of suicide. We both prayed again and agreed in Jesus' name and His authority. We bound and cast out every unholy, ungodly, and unrighteous thing in the house and pled the blood of Jesus over it.

The woman began to weep and praise God. She knew that her God, her Daddy, had heard her and cared. I invited her to meet with my friends and family of believers so we could continue to encourage her and her us. She gave me a powerful word about Satan going before God and asking to sift us like wheat. As I left her home and drove away, I was changed. I felt renewed. I felt the same love from my Daddy that she felt.

Since then I have kept in contact with this person. God continues to move in her life as He does in mine. God used this event to show me that He hears every thought, every cry, and every word. He is the God of answers as He says in Jeremiah 33:3, *"Call out to me and I will answer you."* As I made myself available to Him, even dragging my feet, He revealed that He is in control and ready to answer.

Poison: Christy (mother, business owner)

My son at age three could get into anything and loved any kind of chemical. Nothing seemed to deter him from tasting everything he could get his hands on. One day he poured lighter fluid into a sippy cup. He drank about one-third of it before he realized it was not good and that he was not feeling well. He began to have trouble breathing, and he ran to me. He was choking profusely, and between chokes he screaming that his throat was on fire. He was fighting for every breath. I asked him what he had done. I ran out to the porch where he had been playing, thinking that my son was going to die. I

89

found his sippy cup and lighter fluid on the ground.

I started praying, crying out to God for restoration of lungs, stomach, esophagus and throat. I called 911 and Poison Control. I stuck my fingers down his throat to try to get him to throw up. I did not know that I could have made matters worse by making him vomit.

Poison Control immediately told me not to make him throw up. I said I had to because the fumes were coming up out of his mouth, making it impossible for him to breathe. I had to do something, and I figured if the fumes were inside of him they had to come out. I began to pray while I was still on the phone with the poison control.

The ambulance arrived and took my son to the hospital. The paramedics asked me if he had spoken since the incident happened. I said no. They said that he would have lung and esophagus damage and possibly not be able to speak because of the induced vomiting.

I had already called my husband, and he had alerted a bunch of pastors and prayer warriors to pray for healing and restoration. I also prayed. I know the paramedics thought I was completely nuts, but when it's your child, you don't care what others think.

When we reached the hospital, my son had still said nothing. But suddenly he sat up in his seat. He had never seen the outside of a building as big as the hospital before, and he yelled out, "That is the biggest castle I have ever seen." At that moment I knew God had done a miraculous healing and had restored my son's throat and lungs. I just knew it.

My husband arrived and we both claimed God's word and continued to pray that all results from our child's tests and x-rays would be completely clean. God not only restores, heals, and delivers, but he hears the prayers of His people! My son walked out of the hospital the same day with no signs of any chemical ever being in his body. He had no adverse reactions, no discharges, no medications, no stomach pumping, no stomachaches and no pain. And anyone who knows him today knows that the boy just doesn't stop talking!

Specific Instructions: Jaime (mother, housewife)

It was the first day of school, and as an excited mom, I walked my children to the playground to watch and take pictures of the event. As I stood at the gate, I noticed a mom whose son had been in my son's class the year before. We had been over to their amazing house for a birthday party, and I had spoken to her a few times. I decided to say hello.

We ended up talking until the kids were all gone. We said our goodbyes, and I went on my way. As I left God spoke to me some very specific instructions. God told me, *"You need to get her the book,* Streams in the Desert, *and tell her that I love her. Her husband just left her after she found out about an affair he was having."* I thought, *"No way."* This was the perfect family. They had everything and even talked about God. To be honest, she was very intimidating to me because she seemed so put together.

However, I went to the Christian bookstore and bought the book. I was so nervous. As I drove to the school to pick up the kids, I prayed, "Please God just let it be me and her alone, and I need help." This was way out of my comfort zone!

I pulled up, and there were cars and people all over. I walked to the class to get my son, and she was standing there with no one else around. I took a deep breath, handed her the book, and said, "God told me you needed this book, and He wanted me to tell you that He loves you." She started to cry, and then I started to cry. She went on to tell me how much she needed to hear that. She told me about her husband and the affair. She hadn't told anyone because she was afraid of what people at the school might think. She was able to confide in me and let out some of the confusion and frustration. It was an amazing moment, and we became really good friends after that!

God uses willing vessels. If you are pliable clay, God will shape, mold, and use you wherever you are!

CHAPTER 8

A BITTER STRUGGLE

"Bitterness imprisons life; love releases it."
– Harry Emerson Fosdick

One night not long after my wife had confessed infidelity, I was in the shower, and the enemy started to attack my mind. I started asking Kara questions about the events even though I knew the answers wouldn't help me. Before I knew it, I felt the presence of bitterness within me. I was sitting on our bed with my arms crossed. Kara had been exposed to this before, so she began to pray for me. She took authority over the spirit of bitterness, but I was not ready to let go of it. I felt the increasing rage coming, and my whole body began to get hot. I knew what I had to do, but I was being disobedient and rebellious.

I could feel the darkness closing in around me. I felt a strong desire to let the bitterness take over and control me. At that moment I heard God tell me to stand up and fight. He showed me a picture of a sword and told me to take it and use it against the enemy. Then the Lord showed me a picture of the spirit of bitterness. It was a mass of tentacles with darkness in the middle, where there was a twisted and deformed face. It was an ugly and menacing-looking being. The Lord spoke to me again and told me that he had given me the strength to fight. He told me not to let the enemy win. He told me not to give up.

It was at that moment that I decided to fight. I gathered the strength God made available to me, looked at Kara, and said, "I choose to forgive you." I had battled with bitterness a few times before, and it was at this point each time that I would feel the bitterness in me. This time was no different. As soon as I said those words, I felt a tightening in my stomach. An intense strain inside of me was rising from my stomach up into my chest. It made me open my mouth and bend over at the waist. When I was able to regain my breath, I said, "I forgive you, Kara." I experienced an involuntary silent scream, and then I was able to relax.

I then heard the Lord tell me that this fight was not over. In past times after I forgave Kara, that was the end of it. But this time I could feel that God was taking me to a place of total freedom so that I would not have to go through this again. I was led to tell Kara that I released her from my condemnation. As soon as I finished that sentence, I experienced something that I never had before. I heard a loud and terrible voice in my head scream, "Oh no you don't!"

At that moment, my head was jerked so that Kara was in my view, and my eyes involuntarily met hers. I was trying to look away from her, but it did not seem like I was in control. All of a sudden, I saw Kara pushed away from me, and I felt sucked backwards. We did not get physically pushed, but what I saw with my eyes was Kara projected farther away from me as I felt myself getting sucked backward. This only lasted a few seconds because I was able to get my bearings and regain control. I looked at Kara to see a look of absolute terror on her face. She was getting a crash course in dealing with the demonic, and unfortunately it was through me.

Things began to settle down a bit, but I still heard the Lord say to me, "It's not over yet." I sensed that this was a very important battle and that I needed to push through. I really had no idea or sense of leading what to do next, so I just started to repeat, "Kara, I release you from my condemnation and judgment." It was not very long before I felt the strain in the pit of my stomach again.

Kara was sitting on the bed with a look of shock and concern on her face. She did not know what to do. I think she was still praying. I was in agony on the bed as the Lord spoke to me and said, "Deal with the rights." A few weeks prior to this, the Lord had spoken to me about rights that I was holding on to—the right to hold Kara in condemnation, the right to hurt her like she hurt me, the right to hold on to unforgiveness, and the biggest one, the right to hate her. You can see how it would be impossible for me, or anyone, to keep the door shut on bitterness while hanging on to these rights.

I started to repent for holding onto the rights, and there was a whirlwind of response. As I was speaking, the strain inside of me became very intense. It was exhausting. When I got to the "right to hate her," it produced the biggest and most intense response. I spoke the words, and I was jerked forward face-down onto the bed. I started to cough violently, followed by a series of dry heaves. I was sure that I was going to vomit all over the bed. This was followed by about three or four loud, emotional wails as most of my strength left me.

I was sobbing loudly on the bed at that point. The emotional release was incredible, and the joy that followed was unparalleled by anything I have ever experienced. Kara began to relax and to come back down the wall a little. She was crying with me.

The Problem of Conflict and Intimidation

That experience wasn't the first I'd had with bitterness, though it was certainly the most dramatic. Bitterness and me had gotten along pretty well for most of my life. I wasn't very aware of our relationship but it was there nonetheless.

I thought, like many of us do, that I was very good at forgiveness. When someone hurt me, I would say, "It's okay. Don't worry about it." Instead of acknowledging the hurt, I would push it away. Soong-Chan Rah writes in *The Next Evangelicalism,*

Confrontation can lead to discomfort, but confrontation and discomfort can also lead to transformation. After all, without a disturbed sense about ourselves, why would anyone change?

Those of us who struggle, or have struggled, with the fear of confrontation face an unfortunate dilemma. Our hearts can only take so much repressed anger, so eventually there is going to be an explosion. We fight to maintain an illusion of peace when we are out in the world. We don't want anyone to think we might not have it all together. So where do we eventually explode? For many it's at home behind closed doors with those we love the most. This is a very ugly inevitability for those who "brush off" hurts rather than dealing with the emotions involved.

This was my pattern of behavior for many years. It's the reason I felt almost constant turmoil on the inside and very rarely ever felt peace. People close to me felt that they had to "walk on eggshells" around me because my attitude could change so rapidly. I was an angry, bitter adult. When I got married, I carried all of that repressed anger into my marriage and shared it with my wife. When our kids were a few years old, it seemed like they were afraid of me. I never hit them and rarely yelled, but it still seemed that they were afraid of me. I didn't know why.

Are there people in your life who intimidate you? You may never have seen violent behavior from them, but they make you afraid. There is a sense that anything could set them off, and you don't know what they might do. Maybe you are living with that kind of person. What you might be experiencing is someone whose heart is being held captive by a spirit of bitterness. The effect it's having on you is spiritual and not necessarily physical.

I had allowed this spirit into my life, and it made my family afraid of me. It's terrible to feel like your family is afraid of you.

I remember asking myself, "How did I get this way?" I don't recall being a very angry child, but I didn't turn to the perfect love of God when I experienced different hurts in my life. I was an easy target for bitterness. Its grasp on me became greater with every failure to acknowledge hurt and truly forgive. Every emotion other than anger became more repressed. My heart grew cold. Our adversary will take full advantage in the absence of the perfect love of God.

Bitterness Defeated

My freedom from bitterness started with a reconnection to the love from Father God. As I began to forgive myself, God tore off the layers of self-hatred and filled me with His love. It was only then that I could truly begin to forgive and release the many hurts and repressed anger. I have learned that true and lasting forgiveness is impossible without a real connection to the perfect love of God. Forgiveness is a supernatural thing only possible through the power of Jesus.

One day after my Blazer experience, I made an appointment with Operation Light Force to help me deal with bitterness. I had repented of bitterness, and God had cleared a lot of it out of my life, but I needed help for a particular issue. The appointment was progressing nicely until the Holy Spirit showed my prayer minister that there was a "spirit of intimidation" in me. The prayer minister called the spirit out, and when he did this, I experienced a choking sensation in my throat, and it made me cough about three times. What followed the coughing was an intense wave of emotion. It came out in a shrieking wail that resonated throughout the entire building. Everyone in the building heard it. I collapsed sobbing on the floor completely shocked by what had come out of my mouth. Every single bit of my energy was gone, and all I could do was lie there crying and shaking.

One of the prayer ministers told me that when the spirit was called out, my eyes and face changed in a way that terrified her. She said violence and murder were in my eyes, face, and posture.

After a few minutes of lying on the floor, the peace of God began to wash over me and fill me. I knew right then that things were going to be different. My kids were no longer going to be afraid of me, and my wife was not going to have to walk on eggshells.

Another significant breakthrough in my journey out of bitterness came at the fire station one brisk winter night. Get a few firemen or police officers to be honest and you would probably come away with the impression that they don't like people very much. Those of us in these careers constantly see people at their worst. We see people who don't take care of themselves, abuse the system, steal, get hooked on drugs and alcohol, neglect and abuse their children, and commit all sorts of crime. These experiences don't give us the best perspective of the human race.

It's very easy for cops and firemen to stereotype people and become very judgmental. I was stationed at a place where we would go on calls almost non-stop to nursing homes for the silliest things. Sometimes there was a genuine emergency, but many times the staff there called 911 for routine x-rays, blood work, wound dressing changes, foot pain, and other non-emergency events. The reason they would call 911 was because, if they called a private ambulance company, then they would have to wait for an hour or so. When they called 911, we would arrive in minutes. It was maddening at times to be abused because someone didn't want to wait.

A friend of mine joined me at this station to be my partner. When he started at the station, he was a very happy-go-lucky person. After just a few months, he came in one morning and told me that his wife had asked what had happened to him. She told him that he had become so bitter. We laughed about it because I knew exactly what he was talking about.

After experiencing "people" for some time, my statements began to be, "All nursing home personnel are…," "All overweight people are…," "All drug addicts are…," and so on. Those are bitter judgments, and they stand like a fortress in front of compassion. It is impossible to display true compassion if there are bitter judgments alive in us.

If we tell God we need Him in every area of our lives and ask Him to transform us, He will begin to show us areas that need healing and freedom. I began to notice that I was having a hard time showing people love and compassion. I asked the Lord why, and He showed me all of the judgments I had made about people. I discovered that I was holding onto judgments against about seventy-five percent of people in the world. No wonder I was having trouble with love and compassion!

As my eyes were opened, I was grieved and began to repent. I bound critical spirits and judgmental spirits in the name of Jesus and commanded them to leave. I felt a release and then a peace wash over me. Then the Holy Spirit filled me with love and compassion for people. It was very soon after I experienced freedom from bitter judgments that God moved me to a different station and began to move through me in power. God needed me to be clean from all kinds of bitterness before He could begin to move through me in love and power. Love and bitterness cannot co-exist. If there is any bitterness in our hearts, it will come through in the way we live, speak, and minister. We end up condemning people instead of loving them.

According to 1 Corinthians 13 (NIV), if we speak in the tongues of men or of angels, but do not have love, we are only resounding gongs or clanging cymbals. People don't listen to "gongs." People are offended by "gongs." Believe me, I know. I have been a "gong" more than a few times in my life.

More breakthrough for me came when God showed me that bitterness can also come from subtle or unusual avenues. For two years I had I owned a pool service business that I worked on my days off from the Fire Department. I was so tired of it. One of my greatest desires had been to someday have my own business, and God made that happen for me. But now, two years later, my greatest desire was for Him to take it away. I was tired of the headache and the hassle. I was tired of the phone calls and pretty much everything else that had to do with the business.

It was a Wednesday, and I had just gotten back into town the day before from a vacation with Kara. Now I had to go clean pools. I was more irritable and bitter about the business than I had ever been. I was just about done for the day, and my attitude had not improved. All of a sudden my right heel began to hurt. Every time I stepped down on it pain shot through my whole right foot. It felt very swollen, though I could not see any swelling. It was so painful that it reduced me to a limp for the better part of two weeks.

I started to ask some questions about what I was experiencing in my foot and found out that I had what seemed to be plantar fasciitis. The condition is incurable; the only medical option is continuous treatment. It involves steroid injections into the foot and then crutches for a few weeks. After all of that there is no guarantee it won't come back. In fact, it commonly does.

I quickly decided that the continuous treatment plan wasn't going to be an option. I contacted a ministry that had been dealing with the spiritual roots of diseases for twenty years and asked what the possible roots of that affliction were. They told me that one of the roots was bitterness. At first I dismissed it, because there was no one I knew of that I was holding bitterness toward. A few days later, the Lord brought the issue back to my mind and also showed me a picture of the pool service business. The Lord spoke and said that I was holding bitterness against the business. It was like a light-bulb clicked on in my head. That night I confessed the bitterness that I was holding toward the business and commanded any spirit of bitterness to leave. The next day I woke up with only slight pain in my foot. Later on that same day, the pain was completely gone. It has never been back! That is a powerful testimony of what bitterness can do to us if we give it the rights to our hearts. It's also an awesome testimony of the kind of freedom we get through Jesus and the healing that comes with it.

Bitterness Is Poison

The original Greek word for bitterness is *pikria*, meaning poison. Bitterness is poison! Bitterness will rot our souls and kill us from the inside out. I have shared how bitterness affected me and those around me, but the most devastating effect of bitterness was the destruction it caused to my relationship with God.

> But if ye forgive not men their trespasses, neither will your Father forgive your trespasses. — Matthew 6:15

Until I was reconnected to love and finally able to truly forgive, I had disqualified myself from God's forgiveness.

> For I see that you are full of bitterness and captive to sin.
> — Acts 8:23

If we walk with bitterness we will not walk with God. A severe result of bitterness is that it causes the attitude of our heart to grow cold toward God. If we are not able to love others by forgiving them, then we are also unable to love God (1 John 4:20).

> Looking diligently lest any man fail of the grace of God; lest any root of bitterness springing up trouble you, and thereby many be defiled. — Hebrews 12:15

Bitterness defiles us. It was only after I was cleansed from bitterness that I could begin to walk fully in the mandate God has for all of us to reflect who He is to the lost.

My wife and I were ministering freedom one time to a woman who had done a very good job of repressing her anger and emotions. She had been the victim of many traumas and was very damaged by the inability of her father to show her any love and affection. The pain had been pushed down and the emotions stifled so much that she couldn't even feel the pain anymore. But it was killing her from the inside out. The result was a hard and bitter heart.

At the leading of the Holy Spirit, I told her I was going to stand in for her father. This is something we do at the leading of the Holy Spirit, and it can be very powerful. I had the woman stand. I stood in front of her and said her name. That was all it took as the hands of God reached into her and showed her the extent of the pain. She began to break down and wept as God showed her that there was a little girl inside of her, crying out for the affection of her father. As I began to confess on behalf of her father for all of the injustices, traumas and shortcomings, the daughter of God began to shed the scales around her heart and melt under the power of God. Grace and love filled her, and when I asked her to forgive me, she sincerely replied through tears, "I forgive you, Dad." Her heart was alive once again. This is a testimony of past wounds driving a wedge between Father God and us.

Francis Frangipane writes in *The Three Battlegrounds:*

Is your love growing and becoming softer, brighter, more daring, and more visible? Or is it becoming more discriminating, more calculating, less vulnerable, and less available? This is a very important issue, for your Christianity is only as real as your love is. A measurable decrease in your ability to love is evidence that a stronghold of cold love is developing within you.

I encourage you to ask God to show you where there may be bitterness in your heart and then allow Him to set you free.

Questions For Thought

- In what ways has bitterness manifested in your life, actions? Do you tend to operate in blatant rage or passive-aggressive assault?

- In what ways do you struggle to release offenses and forgive others?

- Are you likely to brush off any offenses in an effort to avoid confrontation? Why?

- In what ways do you see bitterness in those around you? Your kids?

- In what areas is God asking you to forgive? Are you ready to do that? (Ask God for help!)

CHAPTER 9

THE POWER OF GOD IS WITH YOU, PART TWO

"If lips and life do not agree, the testimony will not amount to much." – Harry Ironside

A Sidewalk Encounter

It was a warm, sunny day, and I was riding my bike down my street after eating lunch with my kids at school. I was nearing my house when I noticed a familiar man walking toward me on the sidewalk. I recognized him as someone I had been seeing lately walking around the neighborhood. He had just moved in a few houses down from mine. We had never talked, and the past few times I had seen him, he didn't seem too friendly. I was planning on riding right on by with my eyes straightforward. It seemed like we were both doing our best to avoid each other.

My plan was going well until I noticed his shirt out of the corner of my eye. I turned my head so I could get a good look at it as I rode by. I had the exact same shirt, but that wasn't what got my attention. What got my attention was the fact that his shirt was given out by the church I used to go to.

I instantly realized that I had a connection with this man, and as soon as that thought hit me, the Holy Spirit grabbed my heart and brought me to attention. I stopped about ten feet behind him and looked at him as he walked away from me. I heard the soft voice of the Lord: "*I want you to talk to that man.*" I lowered the kickstand on my bike and began to walk after the stranger.

I called out to him and he stopped, turning quickly. He looked a little irritated that he was being interrupted. His hair was disheveled, and a look of consternation played across his face. I was thinking, "*Oh boy, here we go.*" I approached slowly and asked him about his shirt. He told me he got it at the church he went to. I told him I used to go to that same church and that I have that same shirt. From there we explored that connection and introduced ourselves.

We were making small talk, but I could tell he wanted to get back to whatever he was doing, or wherever he was going. The "friendliness" he was able to manage for the small talk was forced, and his eyes reflected a hardness that comes from carrying heavy burdens for way too long.

Our small talk sputtered out, and we would have gone our separate ways, but the Holy Spirit nudged me to ask him if I could pray for him. He told me that I could. I began to pray for this man I knew nothing about.

As I was praying the Lord began to give me a glimpse of the love He had for this man. As the Lord began to show me how He felt about the man, my prayer became God's words of love and adoration. The Lord was telling this man just how much He loved and cared about him through me. Then the Lord began to give me insight into this man's life. I began to speak to the man as the Lord led about the hurts and pains he had experienced. The Lord began to show me different things that had been done to this man and the things this man had done.

The Lord showed me all of the hopelessness that had built up in the man's soul and how desperate he was for something to change. Then the Lord began to speak to me about how He wanted to be the answer for the man and how He could heal the man's broken heart. The Lord showed me that He wanted to take all of the heavy burdens onto His own back and give the man rest. The Lord continued to speak hope, love and life to this man.

I was looking at the man as I was sharing all of the words God was giving to me. The man kept his face down, but as I spoke to him I could see the tears fall. I placed my hand on his shoulder as I spoke, and I could hear him mumbling the word, "wow."

After I spoke everything the Lord gave me, the man raised his head and what I saw brought joy to my soul. His countenance had completely changed. There was no longer consternation on his face or hardness in his eyes. His face lit up with a smile, and his eyes reflected joy and hope. He stood for a moment and then began to tell me about his life and how hopeless everything had seemed. He told me that before he left for his walk, he told God that he needed to hear from Him. He said that he didn't think he could continue on unless he heard from God. He asked God to send someone to speak to him and then I showed up.

We talked for a bit longer and then headed in opposite directions. My heart was full, and I thanked God for using me to speak to my new friend. I was, and continue to be, overwhelmed by the love God wants to pour out onto His precious children.

There's Healing In His Arms: Rachelle (court reporter)

I had been having a lot of female problems that were becoming debilitating in many ways for me. They were affecting every area of my life, including my husband and children. I was entering my third year of these issues.

Our finances were in very bad shape over the first two years, and going to the doctor wasn't an option. In the third year, I finally got to see my doctor. He informed me that I had four polyps in my uterus and a cyst on my ovary. He told me that they needed to come out. He wanted to make sure there was no cancer, and he scheduled me for surgery four days later.

I remember rushing over to the hospital because the blood work had to be done to meet the surgery date he was setting. I sat in the check-in area for hours by myself waiting to get my blood work done. I remember crying and shaking inside and out because I was so afraid. I began to think about my two sons and what life would be like for them without me. I had already been through so much during the past five years that I knew I could not take anything else on my plate. As I sat in the waiting area, I saw a booklet on the table about the Lord. I thought, "I'm not even picking it up because it's probably Jehovah's Witnesses or something else that I just don't need to be dealing with."

The Lord gently nudged me. He said, *"Pick it up. Read it."* So I picked it up and looked at it. There was an article in it that was about Jesus and His love for me—how He was with me, heard me, and knew that I was afraid. I began to feel His peace come over me. I calmed down, and I was able to relax in His love for me.

When I got home that late afternoon, I remember just being broken on my knees before God and crying out to Him. I told Him I didn't think I could take any more physically, emotionally, or spiritually! I begged the Lord to remove this burden from me! I cried out to God saying, "Lord, you say that your yoke is easy and your burden is light." I wept and wept to Him saying, "Lord, my yoke is heavy and my burden is not light. I can't bear this anymore!" After releasing all of these emotions to the Lord, I stood up. I pulled myself together and headed to our home church meeting. I was under such heaviness.

I arrived and was surprised to see about eight or nine people that I didn't know from another home church. All I thought was, "Great! Now what am I to do? I need my home church tonight. I need to share with them what has been going on. I need them to pray for me tonight. I really need them! I can't share anything now. There are too many people here that I don't know!" Little did I know, the Lord had different plans.

We all began to worship together. The Holy Spirit was so strong that night that others began repenting with their faces on the floor, weeping and asking for God's forgiveness. The Lord began to tug at my heart. He was telling me to release everything to Him and to not be afraid!

I was silent for some time with tears rolling down my face. As He pressed on my heart, I confessed with my mouth to the Lord that I will trust in Him with my entire being. I asked Him to forgive me for my fear. I told Him that I would go into that hospital if it was His will and let them do the surgery because I knew I was in His hands. As I released all of my fears to God, He took them from me! He replaced my fear with peace in my spirit.

Later that night, a ten-year-old boy came up to me. He laid his hands on me and prayed over me for healing in my body. Tears were pouring out of his eyes as he cried out to the Lord on my behalf! All I could hear God saying to me was, *This is childlike faith!* I felt broken as a child showed me what real faith in our God looks like. I had never had faith like that before.

When I got home that night, I heard the Lord say to me, *Read My word. Take this time with me. Listen and seek Me. Study Me. Hear Me. Learn Me. Learn what My word says about healing and about who I Am.* So I asked my husband if he would give me some time and let me be. He did.

A couple of days later I knew that I was not going to have the surgery! It was the decision that God put on my heart. I called the hospital and canceled the surgery. I made an appointment with my doctor and told him that I wasn't going to have the surgery. I told him why I wanted to cancel the surgery and what the Lord was doing in my heart. I wasn't prepared for his response. He said to me, "It's no problem, Rachelle. I have seen many miracles, and they do happen. Take the time that you need with the Lord. I would tell you if I thought you had something life-threatening. However, I stand in agreement with you at this time."

Over the next year, I would still get symptoms at certain times of the month. One of the major symptoms was fever or chills that were starting to be there all the time. I went back to my doctor and he ordered some blood work and another ultrasound. The polyps were still there and the cyst on the ovary had grown bigger. The blood results caused my doctor to call me in and set a surgery date. We were leaving to go on a family vacation when the call came in.

As we were traveling, I felt fear trying to creep back up on me. This time I recognized it quickly. The next night I finally shared with my husband that the fevers and the fear had to go. I needed him to pray over me. He did, three different times. Each time he laid his hands on me to pray the fevers would stop! The next day, the fevers would come back. He would pray again and they would go away. I knew this was a deep-rooted spiritual attack on me.

While I was on vacation, the Lord led me to read Beth Moore's book, *Believing God*. It began to really minister to my spirit and awaken my faith to the Word that God was already instilling and teaching me in my heart about healing. We prayed against fear and worshiped the Lord. The fear left and peace stayed with me but the fevers kept trying to hang around.

Shortly after we got home I had to leave again. I got on the plane and there were only two places to sit. I said, "Okay, Lord, help me with this one." I sat down beside a lady and her daughter. We shared back and forth, and then I began to open to her about my four-year health battle. She listened intently and then told me that the Lord had directed her to pray over me. She informed me that she was a pastor's wife out of a church in Texas. I allowed her to pray over me. The woman leaned into my ear as if she were speaking to the enemy and took authority in the name of Jesus against this attack on my body, my ovaries, and my uterus! I knew God was doing something and I held perfectly still. Then she turned to me and began praying over me with such power that I knew without a doubt God used her to come and do spiritual warfare on my behalf!

I felt so different! So good! So excited! I came off that plane like it was a five-minute flight! Everyone around me looked as if they had just been dragged through the mud. I was full of energy and my eyes were beaming with the light of the Lord! The fevers COMPLETELY left me! Permanently! Gone!

Two days after I returned home I had a scheduled doctor's appointment to discuss surgery. When I came in, he did another ultrasound. The polyps were still there. The growing cyst was GONE! Completely gone! He looked at me and said, "There is no need to do surgery. The cyst is gone." God did a miracle in me! I told the doctor, "As far as the polyps go, we will wait to hear what the Lord wants me to do. Not what I want to do." I thank the Lord for his faithfulness to me and His faithfulness to His own Word. God IS GOOD! God is my FATHER and I know my FATHER wants me healed!

If you desire to know what the results are with the polyps – you can email me at *mjrefuge@gmail.com*. This month is July 2012 and we believe God has removed the polyps from me! We will know more when He leads us to go back to the doctor for a follow-up in the future!

Bibles and Open Doors: Jon (sales manager)

When the new general manager showed up to take over the local branch of a large national company, I was already a regular visitor. The new manager and I hit it off right away and developed a friendship. I continued to visit him at the branch. At the time, I owned a promotional products business.

My new friend laid out some conversational rules for me. If he asked me questions about God, I could talk to him about God. If he didn't ask me questions about God, then I was not to talk to him about God. Over the next couple of months, I only talked about God a few times.

One day he surprised me. He said he wanted me to buy him a Bible. I asked him if he was serious. I knew that he made a very good living as the general manager and that he could buy his own Bible if he wanted one. Nevertheless, I went to the Christian bookstore, purchased a new leather-bound New King James Bible, and delivered it to him at his office.

On another visit I noticed that the Bible I had bought was nowhere in sight. I asked him what happened to the Bible, and he said he didn't know. He thought his branch manager took it. He asked if I would buy him another Bible.

Without hesitation I walked out of his office, drove to the Christian bookstore, and bought him another Bible just like the first one. I drove to his office, opened up the box, and handed it to him.

One day I decided to visit my friend unannounced. I walked into his office and discovered that the Bible I had given him was open on his office table. I commented that I was happy that he was reading it.

My friend had told me many times that he wanted me to come work for him as a sales representative. But I always told him that I was perfectly happy working for myself selling promotional products. He steadily climbed the corporate ladder and settled into a very prominent position in the corporate office. Some time later, my business was in a lot of trouble as we lost our national account and most of our other customers who were tied to the home-building industry. For three years, my wife and I put everything we had into rebuilding our business, but it wasn't going well.

One day I speed-dialed a customer, and to my surprise, my friend answered the phone. It had been a while since we had spoken. He asked me how things were going, and I shared with him my frustration with not being able to resurrect my business and save my house from foreclosure.

He asked me again to come and be a sales representative for his company. He said, "I want you to stroll into the office the way you always do and tell the general manager that you are going to be putting in your resume." I said I would call him. My friend said, "That isn't what I told you to do." He repeated his instructions. I got in my car, drove to the office, and followed my friend's instructions.

A month later, right on time as both our other major accounts collapsed, I was able to transition into my present job. I am now enjoying my career as the commercial sales manager of the local branch.

God led me to buy two Bibles, and out of my obedience an amazing relationship was birthed. I could see how the Bibles were blessing my friend, but I had no idea how God would use that relationship to rescue my family and me when we were drowning. Now I am a living testimony in my company, and God has been working through me ever since!

CHAPTER 10
BE TRANSFORMED

"Do not gloat over me, my enemy! Though I have fallen, I will rise.
Though I sit in darkness, the LORD will be my light."
– Micah 7:8 *(NIV)*

Transformation is a life-changing reconnection to the perfect love of God. I could not allow God to use me to reach others or build any testimonies for the advancement of His kingdom until I allowed Him to transform me. He birthed me into a new creation (2 Cor. 5:17). I was dead and ineffective until I cried out in desperation for God to awaken my soul and to renew me in His love. Only as I was being set free from the bondage holding me captive did the Holy Spirit begin to manifest in and through me, allowing those around me to see His light. As I continue to put one foot in front of the other on this journey God has for me, He is faithful in showing me the dirt in my soul, and as it's cleansed, the light in me gets brighter. He has rescued me from the grave and given me a seat in the heavenly places (Eph. 2:5-6).

And be not conformed to this world: but be ye transformed by the renewing of your mind, that ye may prove what is that good, and acceptable, and perfect, will of God. — Romans 12:2

The Greek word for "transformed" is *metamorphoo*. It means, "changed by something." It's not something that we can make happen. To be transformed seems to mean being completely changed by an outside force.

As I consider my journey of transformation, four elements stand out as essential. They are:

- Desperation
- Repentance
- Deliverance
- Wilderness Experiences

Desperation

We must come to a place of complete desperation. Over the years I have recognized two different types of desperation.

The first says, "I can't live like this anymore. My circumstances are too much for me to handle." I have experienced this type to be initiated by circumstances, and the associated desperation is one that says, "Just help me through this hard time, and I will be on my way."

The second type says, "I can't live one more day without being totally saturated with the presence of God, and I am willing to give up everything to get it." I have seen both types while meeting different people in crisis. I have seen those with the second type of desperation get set free while those with the first type stay in chains. God knows our hearts and will not be mocked (Gal. 6:7).

It's only in our desperation for a total heart change that we can see the dark areas of our heart and invite God in to heal them. We must be ready to put the deeds of the body to death. If we don't, we won't ever live (Rom. 8:13).

I remember ministering to a man who came to us broken and ready to be healed. He had recognized his need for God to saturate and change his entire life. As we sat with him and listened for God the Lord showed me a vision. Jesus had a shovel and was digging in the man's backyard. There were a number of holes spread around the yard. Then the Lord spoke and said, "There are things in your past that you have buried deep in your heart. You have been unwilling to face them. It's time to uncover those things so I can heal your heart.

114

You won't have to do it alone as I will be right there with you giving you the help and strength you need."

Desperation is not about how many religious activities we can be a part of. Religiosity seeks to wear a holy mask while keeping our hearts and lives in the status quo. To truly surrender our hearts means to place everything in our lives on the altar, even the parts we don't want to look at. The things we have buried deep in our hearts need to be unearthed before they can be healed. That type of surrender is motivated by coming to the end of ourselves.

True desperation is impossible without humility. It takes much humility to give up our lives. The pride in our hearts will deceive us, telling us that we don't need to give up anything (Obad. 1:3). Pride will tell us that we are doing just fine. But the proud will never experience the fullness and intimacy of God because God will resist them (James. 4:6).

Francis Frangipane writes,

Pride is the armor of darkness itself.

As long as we wear pride, every attempt God makes to transform our hearts will be thwarted. The proud despise correction and resist refinement. Transformation is unobtainable to those who are desperate to keep their pride, and they become an abomination to the Lord (Prov. 16:5). The ears of the proud are closed to instruction and become deaf to the Holy Spirit. The light that the proud think they have is actually darkness (Luke 11:35).

We must recognize the pride in our hearts. We must be willing to submit to God in humility. The tools needed to resist our adversary only come with humility (James. 4:6-7). The road of transformation is marked by a lifestyle of humility.

And Jesus said unto him, Go thy way; thy faith hath made thee whole. And immediately he received his sight, and followed Jesus in the way. — Mark 10:52

When I read this passage, I almost skipped over it, but something caught my attention. This passage describes a blind man lying beside the road outside of Jericho. Jesus is on His way out of the city and walks by this man. A few verses earlier, it says that as soon as the man heard it was Jesus walking by, the man cried out to Him. He cried out to Jesus in faith because he knew Jesus could heal him. The man's faith was already there before Jesus was there in the flesh.

I know many of us have heard this story many times, but it's not the specific miracle that caught my attention this time. What did was the sequence of events. This man cried out to Jesus in faith, and Jesus said, "Thy faith has made you whole." The word "whole" is the Greek word *sozo* or *sode-zo*. It means "save, heal, preserve, deliver, protect, do well, be whole." Jesus told the man he was "whole," and then the man received his sight and followed Jesus.

This man was desperate for Jesus! When Jesus told the man he was "whole," I don't think Jesus was talking about physical healing, but instead I think He was talking about the man's soul. Because of the man's great faith demonstrated by the act of crying out, there was an outward manifestation of healing. Then because of the desperation for Jesus already in the man's heart prior to Jesus getting there, the man followed Jesus after the miracle.

The significance of this story isn't necessarily the physical healing. It may have everything to do with the condition and desperation of our hearts as we interact with our Daddy. Are we coming to God desperate and one hundred percent dependent? Or are we coming to Him like the religious leaders:

These people honor me with their lips, but their hearts are far from me. — Matthew 15:8 (NIV)

I was spending some time in the book of Mark one morning, and I came across another story I have heard many, many times. It's one of Jesus' most well-known miracles, the feeding of the five thousand. Something struck me as I read it this time. (We need to ask God to unveil deeper truths and revelations as we read through stories we may have known all of our lives.) The mass of people had been out in the wilderness with Jesus so long that the disciples asked Jesus to send the people away so they could get something to eat. Jesus did not send them away. He fed them.

We find a similar story a little later on. Jesus was with a mass of people, about four thousand, and we are told that they had not eaten for three days. Jesus realized that many of them had come from far away and that if they left with no food, they might faint on the way back. Jesus fed them. As I read these stories, I found the following principle to be true. If we come to Jesus with a desperation that says, "I am willing to give up everything, including what the natural says my body needs to survive, to be with Jesus," then we will not leave hungry!

> Blessed are they which do hunger and thirst after righteousness: for they shall be filled. — Matthew 5:6

Jesus will never send a desperate soul away hungry. These people who stayed with Jesus out in the wilderness didn't leave hungry. I say "stayed" because we don't know how many people were out there originally. All we know is how many were fed. Not everyone is willing to deny himself or herself to be with Jesus. Not everyone is that desperate. It would be very interesting to know how big the group was the first day. I find it interesting that Jesus could have fed the people at any time, but the first time he chose to wait until the day was "far spent," and the second time he waited three days. Jesus is looking for the desperate. Jesus is looking for those who love him enough to get uncomfortable. Those people left their jobs, families, food, plans, and everything else to be with Jesus. That's the heart God is looking for. That's the heart that gets transformed. Transformation is dependent upon our choice to forsake all else to be with our Daddy. How sad for those who left early because they were uncomfortable. They missed out on being miraculously filled by Jesus.

Do we want God to change our circumstances, or do we want God to change us? Do we ask for His help and when He gives it forget about Him until the next time? Do we come to God with

control or ready to give up control? Do we start the journey with
Jesus strong, but fade when things get tough? How many times
have we chosen to "leave" because it got too uncomfortable for
our theology, comfort zone, or physical desires? I've been guilty
more than once.

Repentance

True desperation for Jesus will bring us to our glaring need for
repentance. God will show us the sin in our hearts if we are willing
to acknowledge them. Since sin separates us from God (Isa. 59:2),
we need to acknowledge and deal with any sin He shows us. We
must ask the Lord to reveal to us the iniquities in our hearts like
David did (Ps. 139:23-24).

Jesus began his ministry with a message of repentance (Matt.
4:17). John the Baptist preached repentance (Matt. 3:2). Peter
began his ministry with a message of repentance (Acts 2:38). And
John teaches us to continue a lifestyle of repentance (1 John 1:9).

To repent means *to turn away*. We must turn away from our
lifestyles of sin, and we must boldly approach the throne of grace
with confidence so that we can find mercy (Heb. 4:16).

There was a time when I was asking God to break my heart for
what breaks His. Be careful what you ask for! One night shortly
after I prayed that prayer, we were at our small group meeting
enjoying an especially sweet and intimate time of worship.
Suddenly God answered my prayer, and I was overwhelmed by
sorrow. It fell on me like a ton of bricks, and before I knew it, I
was face down on the floor sobbing. I was completely undone. It
felt like the power of all the grief and unimaginable sadness was
going to rip me apart. It wasn't painful, but it quickly became far
more than my body could handle.

It got so intense that I asked the Lord to take His hand off of me.
He spoke to me and said, *"This is just a glimpse of how sin breaks
My heart."* But it wasn't just sin in general that He was speaking
to me about. It was MY sin. He was showing me how my sins
affected Him. I couldn't lift my face off of the floor. I began to tell

Him how sorry I was. I began to repent for everything He was showing me. I was a complete mess. But in the midst of all of that, there was absolutely no condemnation. There was so much love saturating me. I heard the Lord say, *"I have forgiven you and washed you clean."* I knew without any doubt that the love God had for me in that moment, and forever, was far greater than I will ever understand.

A cry for desperate repentance began to swell in my heart, and I began to speak to the group through sobs. I tried my best to put what God was doing in my heart into words. I was desperate for them to understand how much weight our actions carry. Our sinful choices separate us from God, but His mercy and love beckons for us to remove the wall between us—to close the door to sin. Repentance is the way back into His arms (Acts 3:19). As D.L. Moody put it,

> Man is born with his back toward God. When he truly repents, he turns right around and faces God. Repentance is a change of mind, a change of heart, and it results in a change of action.

Deliverance

> If you do what is right, will you not be accepted? But if you do not do what is right, sin is crouching at your door; it desires to have you, but you must rule over it. — Genesis 4:7 (NIV)

Sin is crouching at the door of our hearts waiting to rule over us. Jesus is knocking at that same door (Rev. 3:20). Because we all have sinned, we all have exposed our hearts to our adversary, thus becoming slaves to sin (Rom. 3:23, 6:17).

Repentance slams the door to sin shut. But we still need to evict the strongman—the demonic spirit holding us captive (Luke 11:15-23). Jesus came to bind up the brokenhearted and to set the captives free (Isa. 61:1). He gave us the authority to trample on the heads of snakes and scorpions in His name (Mark 16:17; Luke 10:19).

Where there is hopelessness, there is captivity. Where there is habitual sin, the enemy is ruling. But God is in the business of exposing our areas of captivity so that we can be free! We need to take the initiative. Paul was addressing the church when he taught them that the weapons of our warfare are not carnal (of flesh and blood) but are mighty for the pulling down of strongholds (2 Cor. 10:4). Paul was teaching the church how to defeat the enemy because they were still being held captive in different areas of their lives. Strongholds protect our adversary's hold on us. It's important that we understand what a stronghold consists of so that we can understand how to pull it down.

To illustrate this, let's consider a child who is abused in some way. Our adversary takes that opportunity to tell the child just how worthless, dirty, and unlovable he is. He tells the child that what happened is his fault. He tells the child that he should never forgive the abuser, that hate is okay, and that people are not trustworthy. As that child grows, he sees more betrayal and pain. All this time the initial lies become more and more ingrained, and the strongholds gain strength. The demonic spirits whispering the lies are well protected because the child is in agreement with them.

Let's consider a less extreme illustration. Consider a teenage girl who has grown up in the church. One day she watches a TV show about rape and feels fear and anxiety begin to grip her. She doesn't have an understanding of how to combat the enemy, so the fear goes unchecked. The spirit of fear begins to tell her that she is going to be raped, and she starts looking over her shoulder everywhere she goes. Her trust in God has begun to crumble, and she starts to fear being alone. The stronghold of fear has been erected. Over the course of time, our adversary makes sure that she sees rapes and assaults on TV, and he entices her to watch movies in which these things happen. The strongholds are reinforced, and the fear evolves into every other area of her life. She finds herself needing medication to control her anxiety. Her trust in God has been defeated.

Consider kids who act out in violence and hear the enemy tell them that violence is appropriate and necessary; overweight kids who hear they are disgusting and will never change; those who have premarital sex and hear that God will never forgive them; drug users who hear they are hopeless and worthless; kids who see kidnappings on TV and hear that it will happen to them; those who find success in their career and hear that they are nothing without it; those who are emotional and hear that emotions equal weakness; kids who sneak a piece of candy and hear that stealing isn't a big deal; those who tell a "little white lie" and hear that it's okay to fib. Consider murderers, thieves, and child molesters who hear that they are beyond any chance of redemption and that they are better off dead.

Our adversary is a roaring lion searching for anyone he can destroy, using anything he can to gain access to us (1 Pet. 5:8). Peter tells us to be "alert" and "vigilant," and so we must be!

Paul states that the weapons of our warfare are not carnal (physical or of the flesh), but that they are mighty *for the pulling down of strongholds.* Typically the weapons we tend to use as believers are very carnal and ineffective against the strongholds of the enemy. We attempt to fight our problems using the world's weapons. Did we forget that Satan is the ruler of this world (John 12:31)? The world and its systems are under the control of Satan and are going to be ineffective against demonic strongholds. They will, most likely, push us even further into his grasp.

For example, anxiety medication doesn't fix fear. It just chemically sedates the body. Traditional counseling may be helpful in exposing some lies, but it offers nothing that is effective in pulling those lies down, and most of the time, medication is used to facilitate the desired response. Yoga doesn't fix stress, it just allows a temporary sense of euphoria while participating in it. (For more about this, read *Exposing the Dangers of Martial Arts and Yoga* by Dr. Vito Rallo.) If it is carnal, it is going to be ineffective against the real issues.

But the weapons of our warfare are not tailored toward the outward manifestations of our issues. Our weapons are designed to destroy the things we can't see. Our weapon is the Sword of the Spirit, and it is designed for the destruction of lies, deceptions, false teachings, false doctrines (Eph. 6:17; Heb. 4:12). We are to assault the strongholds of lies with truth. The Sword of the Spirit is the word of God. It is truth! It is impossible for God to lie (Heb. 6:18). Jesus said that those who know the truth will be free (John 8:32). Satan is the "father of lies," and so his strongholds are destroyed by truth (John 8:42). The truth we need to pull down demonic strongholds is revealed to us by the Holy Spirit, as He is the "Spirit of Truth who guides us into all truth" (John 16:13).

We pull down the lie that we are unforgiveable with the truth of God's forgiveness (Isa. 1:18; 1 John 1:9; Ps. 103:12). We pull down the lie that we are unlovable with the truth of God's love (Zeph. 3:17; John 3:16; Rom. 5:8, 8:37-39; Gal. 2:20; 1 John 4:9). We pull down fear with the truth of God's protection and promises to be for us (Ps. 91; 1 John 4:18; Rom. 8:15, 8:28-29). The truth of God will pull down every stronghold and will disarm the strongman. He can then be cast out in the name of Jesus as you erect a stronghold of truth to guard your heart (Ps. 18:2).

When the stronghold has been destroyed, we must deal with the strongman. The strongman is revealed by its nature. If you are battling fear, then you need to evict the strongman of fear. It you are struggling with bitterness, then the name of the strongman you need to evict is bitterness.

I must stress the importance of making sure to ask the Holy Spirit to fill the areas vacated by the enemy. Once the strongman is evicted, he will come back to see if the place he left has been occupied by the Holy Spirit. If it hasn't, then he will bring seven more spirits, and you will be much worse off (Matt. 12:43-45).

Francis Frangipane writes,

Victory begins with the name of Jesus on your lips; but it will not be consummated until the nature of God is in your heart.

We are continually becoming liberated as we acknowledge sin, repent, pull down the strongholds, evict the strongman, and invite the Holy Spirit to fill us. Paul again addresses the war we are all involved in with his letter to the church in Ephesus.

> Put on the whole armor of God, that ye may be able to stand against the wiles of the devil. For we wrestle not against flesh and blood, but against principalities, against powers, against the rulers of the darkness of this world, against spiritual wickedness in high places. Wherefore take unto you the whole armor of God, that ye may be able to withstand in the evil day, and having done all, to stand. Stand therefore, having your loins girt about with truth, and having on the breastplate of righteousness; And your feet shod with the preparation of the gospel of peace; Above all, taking the shield of faith, wherewith ye shall be able to quench all the fiery darts of the wicked. And take the helmet of salvation, and the sword of the Spirit, which is the word of God — Ephesians 6:11-17

We must not close our eyes or put our heads in the sand. God's people who lack knowledge are in danger of being destroyed (Hosea 4:6). We must seek to know the truth and acknowledge it. Certainly our adversary has acknowledged his war against us (1 Pet. 5:9).

Wilderness Experiences

> In that day, declares the Lord, you will call me 'my husband'; you will no longer call me 'my master'. — *Hosea 2:16 (NIV)*

Transformation requires a walk through the wilderness. The wilderness is a place of preparation. It's the place where we are shaped by the potter's hand. The wilderness offers the chance to choose a new way in the face of difficult trials and tribulations.

But it's a hard place because it's where our old nature begins to die and holiness is birthed in our hearts. Many times it's a place of loss as the kingdom of God replaces the world we have become comfortable with.

For a long time I resisted the wilderness because of pride, fear, selfishness, and idolatry. I was too prideful to be broken, and I feared what would happen to me if I gave up control. For the most part, I only cared about myself, and I loved other things more than God. That's the same attitude Israel (represented by Gomer) had in the book of Hosea as they chased money, power, sex, comfort, and every other idol in the world. In their limited sight, they had so much. In reality, they had nothing.

God allowed all that they had to be taken away. God says in Hosea 2 that He allowed their feasts and parties to end, their luxuries to be stripped away and destroyed, their money to be stolen and their nakedness (shame) to be exposed before everyone. Yet they still stood there with their feet firmly planted and resisted the wilderness.

As I considered all of the things my idols had provided for me, I began to realize that, like the Israelites, I had nothing! I worked overtime at the fire department for more money, but I didn't ever have any extra. I owned a pool business to strive for extra money, but I stilled lived paycheck to paycheck. I had many luxuries that required monthly payments and commitments, but I always faced the increasing likelihood that I was not going to be able to pay all of the bills. I exercised and worked out to keep my body in shape, but it never enabled me to truly love and accept myself. I went to church, attended small group meetings, and read my Bible, but I realized that I had never experienced a close, intimate, real love relationship with my Daddy God. I had nothing.

Do you drive and strive, but never feel like you're gaining any ground? We get promoted, make more money, buy bigger things, get more "religious," get the girl, and yet the unbearable emptiness is still there.

Even with all of this, we would still rather find comfort in our current circumstances than step out into the wilderness. Why? What is so scary about the wilderness? That's where God is! Hosea chapter two gives us such a beautiful picture of the wilderness. God says that the wilderness is where He will "speak comfortably" to us.

7-11-19 *Just what I wrote about! I'm just playing it safe.*

BE TRANSFORMED

The wilderness is where we get purged, refined, and made clean. Those things can and most likely will be very painful, but God is there. God never leaves. In fact, unless we go into the wilderness, we will never be intimate with God. Hosea two says that it's in the wilderness where we begin to call God "Husband" (Ishi) and no longer "Lord" (Baali). What better picture of intimacy is there than that? But it's only available if we are willing to go through the wilderness. God says it's in the wilderness where He will establish us and begin to give back what we have lost. This is what God says happens in the wilderness:

> There I will give her back her vineyards, and will make the Valley of Achor (trouble) a door of hope. There she will sing as in the days of her youth, as in the day she came up out of Egypt. "In that day," declares the LORD, "you will call me 'my husband'; you will no longer call me 'my master.' I will remove the names of the Baals from her lips; no longer will their names be invoked. In that day I will make a covenant for them with the beasts of the field and the birds of the air and the creatures that move along the ground. Bow and sword and battle I will abolish from the land, so that all may lie down in safety. I will betroth you to me forever; I will betroth you in righteousness and justice, in love and compassion. I will betroth you in faithfulness, and you will acknowledge the LORD. "In that day I will respond," declares the LORD— "I will respond to the skies, and they will respond to the earth; and the earth will respond to the grain, the new wine and oil, and they will respond to Jezreel. I will plant her for myself in the land; I will show my love to the one I called 'Not my loved one.' I will say to those called 'Not my people,' 'You are my people'; and they will say, 'You are my God.'" — Hosea 2:15-23 (NIV)

But we resist the wilderness. We turn our back on those promises. Our pride and fear holds us fast. Unless we humble ourselves and crawl into the wilderness on our knees, we will live our whole lives disconnected from our Daddy. The only path to the Promised Land runs through the wilderness. Depending on our willingness, the wilderness can be a direct route to the Promised

Land, or it can include forty years of circles.

Some of us enter the wilderness and then, for whatever reason, decide it's not what we want. The trials overtake us, and instead of letting Jesus be the light to our path, we get lost in the darkness (Ps. 119:105). We don't have to wander lost in the dark like Israel did. Israel wandered as a result of disobedience (Josh. 5:6). If we are obedient, we will find the path God has for us, and it will lead to the Promised Land. We have to get out of our current, destructive circumstances before we can truly find "Ishi."

Though the wilderness offers much uncertainty and possible heartache, we must *rely* on the perfect love of God, who promises to work all things for our benefit (1 John 4:16; Rom. 8:28). Even though we may not *feel* His all consuming love and passion for us in every single step in the wilderness, He promises that He will always be on our side and will never, ever turn His back on us (Heb. 13:5). We trust that the trials God allows in our lives have purpose and that, whatever the trial may be, God's desire is to use it to work out something very special in us (Rom. 5:3-5), to bring us into a more perfect reflection of Jesus (2 Cor. 3:18). A beautiful promise awaits those of us who take courage and continue to persevere:

> The poor and needy search for water, but there is none; their tongues are parched with thirst. But I the LORD will answer them; I, the God of Israel, will not forsake them. I will make rivers flow on barren heights, and springs within the valleys. I will turn the desert into pools of water, and the parched ground into springs. I will put in the desert the cedar and the acacia, the myrtle and the olive. I will set junipers in the wasteland, the fir and the cypress together, so that people may see and know, may consider and understand, that the hand of the LORD has done this, that the Holy One of Israel has created it. — Isaiah 41:17-20 (NIV)

Sometimes we feel stuck in the wilderness. What do you see now as you look at your life? Are you barely able to stand? Are you looking at desolation, hopelessness, despair, loneliness, and emptiness? Is there rubble all around you? Do you feel like you are in the wilderness all by yourself? Is the pain too much for you? Do you want to run and hide? Are you angry with God? Do you feel like He led you out into the middle of nowhere? Were you expecting things to get better, and everything seems to have gotten worse? Do you wonder where God is and where His promises are?

There have been times in my journey with God that I have felt abandoned. There have been times when I felt like it was impossible for me to move forward. I remember times when I knew what God wanted to do in my life but it seemed like there was a huge mountain blocking my path, and I couldn't get past it.

What's going on when we feel like this? Did God bring us out into the wilderness only to leave us to suffer and die? Israel accused Him of that when they were in the desert (Exod. 16:2-3). Does God turn His back on us and refuse to help us when we need Him the most, or is it something else entirely? Is it God who has brought us to a standstill, or have we done it to ourselves?

Let's take a look at the following passage from Isaiah:

"Woe to the obstinate children," declares the LORD, "to those who carry out plans that are not mine, forming an alliance, but not by my Spirit, heaping sin upon sin; who go down to Egypt without consulting me; who look for help to Pharaoh's protection, to Egypt's shade for refuge. But Pharaoh's protection will be to your shame, Egypt's shade will bring you disgrace." — Isaiah 30:1-3 (NIV)

In this passage God is rebuking Judah for looking to Egypt for help when they should have been looking to God. This passage is very relevant to us, as I believe Egypt refers to the "world" and its systems. When we feel stuck and alone in the wilderness, I believe we should remember this passage and ask ourselves one very important question: "Am I going to the world and its systems for my help, or am I going to God?"

Turning to the world can certainly seem like a more attractive option, especially since the world specializes in instant gratification and instant relief from pain through an assortment of avenues.

In the passage above, the Lord says that the counsel from Egypt (the kingdom of the world) will lead us to shame and confusion. Are your choices bringing you peace and abundant life regardless of circumstances like Jesus promised (John 14:27, 10:10)? Or are your choices bringing even more shame and confusion into your life?

In every situation we have an opportunity to take the counsel of God or turn to the world for our answers. We can't have it both ways. If you take counsel from the world, you are making a rebellious choice against the counsel of God. I think we can all agree that God doesn't want to share us with the world (Matt. 6:24).

The world can seem like a better option, but let's remember a few things.

- It's the wilderness where Father speaks comfortably to us and where we can come to know Him in true intimacy (Hosea 2:14, 16).
- He will never leave us or forsake us (Heb. 13:5).
- He offers us great courage if we accept it (Josh. 1:7).
- He never forgets His promises and is always with us (Hag. 2).
- He will strengthen us to do the work He has called us to do (Hag. 1).
- We will never face anything beyond what we have the ability to conquer through Jesus (1 Cor. 10:13).

If we are faithful in putting all of our hope and trust in our Father, the work that He will erect in our lives will be so much more fulfilling, glorious, amazing, joyful, and healing than anything that has ever come before (Rom. 8:28)!

Sometimes when we've been in the wilderness for a while, it seems that it would be easier to move backward instead of forward into what God has for us. We remember better times in our lives when we knew that God was with us. We remember when we could feel and see the blessings of God in our lives. We think, *"If I could just get back to that, then things would be better."*

Does God want to take us back to the past, or does He want to constantly be doing a new work in our lives? If God wants to continually change us from "glory to glory" (2 Cor. 3:18), trying to get back to the past will cause us to miss everything that God wants to do in our lives. No matter where we are, we have not "peaked" in the kingdom of God. Even if we were moving in the Spirit, walking in the anointing, and seeing God move through us daily in the past, God still wants to do a new thing in our lives. He wants to take us to higher and higher levels today and in the future! Here is the promise of God:

> The glory of this latter house shall be greater than the former and in that place I will give peace! — Haggai 2:9

Can we live in peace if we are living in the past? The answer is no. As followers of Jesus, we are to forget the ways and deeds of our fleshly past and become a new creation formed in the nature and spirit of Christ (Eph. 4:22-24). We are to forget that which lies behind us and press on toward Jesus Christ, who reigns ahead of us (Phil. 3:13-14).

I have been in the wilderness, and I have found that the promises of God are true! The work God has done and is doing in me is so much greater than anything in my past, and He continues to do a new thing in me daily.

The wilderness can be scary. It can challenge what we have held to be true our entire lives. It can challenge who we thought we were. But if we can lay those things down and allow Father to take us on a journey, the longing and void that has nagged us will be filled. That's what transformation is, and Jesus said everyone must be transformed to enter His kingdom (John 3:3; Matt. 18:3).

Are You Being Transformed?

I read an article about being "born again" in which the author said that someone who has been truly "born again" can tell you that there has been a dramatic change in their life and attitude, but the person is unable to really describe a specific event or tell you exactly how it happened. That really made sense to me as I thought about how I have been changing.

For most of my life, the phrase "born again" was well known, but there was no revelation of emotion or sense of reality that came with it. I had no idea what it meant or how it felt to be born again.

It wasn't until I began to compare my life as it was to my life as it is now that I began to grasp how different I've become. The more I refused to be conformed to the world, the more I have been conformed into the image of Christ (Rom. 12:2, 8:29). Along the way the Lord has used some experiences to really open my eyes as to how much He has changed me.

This change doesn't mean that I don't sin anymore or that I have come close to perfection. Let me try to explain what has happened to me by telling you about some experiences I've had.

I know that sin is sin and that God sees all sin as the same. However, many of us carry our own scales that say which sins are weightier than others. I had come a long way in my ability to view all sin as weighing the same, but there was a revelatory piece missing in the way I applied that view to my life.

One evening I was meditating on the Lord, and something I had done came to my mind. It was a sin that would never previously have registered as something for which I would need to repent. It was, in my mind, a little sin, and in the past it would have never been on my grid for repentance. Not only did the Lord bring this sin to my mind and show me my need for repentance, but my heart was wrecked and wounded because of it. I thought in that moment, *"When did this happen? When did I start feeling this way?"* I recognized in that moment that I wasn't the same person in my heart, soul, mind, will, and emotions that I used to be. To be honest, and this is kind of funny, I felt sort of violated. I felt as if someone had snuck in and changed who I was into someone else. The sensation was very strange. I loved the change, but it felt very weird.

Another example is the change in my relationship with my son. As a result of past wounds, I had allowed some walls to be erected in my heart. I have already talked about some of the main walls in my heart which were unloving, fear, and bitterness. Those blocks prevented me from really understanding how to love my son and from being able to just rest and enjoy my relationship with him. But as God began to unravel those hurts and heal the wounds, something began to change. The walls guarding my heart began to crumble, and I suddenly became aware of how much I had begun to enjoy my son. We spent more time together and started to bond. I found that I was laughing more around him and was really interested in the things he said and did. The pressure I felt to try and push him to do things or try things evaporated, and I was left with peace. It was a dramatic change that occurred without any extra fasting, praying, Bible reading, or churchgoing. I'm not saying these things aren't important. My point is that I didn't do anything extra to try and make a change happen.

As I was processing these things, the Lord brought to me Romans 12:2. Paul says, "Be transformed."

> And be not conformed to this world: but be ye transformed by the renewing of your mind, that ye may prove what is that good, and acceptable, and perfect, will of God. — Romans 12:2

Are you being transformed or are you being conformed to the world? This question deserves some serious contemplation. The testimony of someone who is being transformed goes far beyond a simple confession of belief. Paul explains in Romans 10:19, "If thou shalt *confess with thy mouth the Lord Jesus, and shalt believe in thine heart* that God hath raised him from the dead, thou shalt be saved." (emphasis added).

We begin the journey of transformation by confessing with our mouth AND believing in our hearts. Jesus teaches us that the mouth speaks what is in our hearts (Luke 6:45; Matt. 12:34). The main focus is on our hearts. If our hearts aren't standing with Jesus, then we are unable to make a true confession with our mouths. If we try to confess Jesus is Lord without surrendering our hearts to Him, then we will be nothing more than hypocrites. Our actions won't be able to back up our words. We might have a "form of godliness," but we deny the power of God to change our hearts (2 Tim. 3:5).

Jesus mentions "fruit" forty-six times in Matthew through John, and each time it refers to the testimony of who His children really are. Jesus said that His children will produce "good fruit." But what is this "fruit?"

> But the fruit of the Spirit is love, joy, peace, patience, kindness, goodness, faithfulness, gentleness, and self-control. Against such things there is no law. — Galatians 5:22-23 (NIV)

The first of those, love, gets a whole chapter in 1 Corinthians:

> If I speak in the tongues of men and of angels, but have not love, I am only a resounding gong or a clanging cymbal. If I have the gift of prophecy and can fathom all mysteries and all knowledge, and if I have a faith that can move mountains, but have not love, I am nothing. If I give all I possess to the poor and surrender my body to the flames, but have not love, I gain nothing. Love is patient, love is kind. It does not envy, it does not boast, it is not proud. It is not rude, it is not self-seeking, it is not easily angered, it keeps no record of wrongs. Love does not delight in evil but rejoices with the truth. It always protects, always trusts, always hopes, always perseveres. Love never fails. But where there are prophecies, they will cease; where there are tongues, they will be stilled; where there is knowledge, it will pass away. For we know in part and we prophesy in part, but when perfection comes, the imperfect disappears. When I was a child, I talked like a child, I thought like a child, I reasoned like a child. When I became a man, I put childish ways behind me. Now we see but a poor reflection as in a mirror; then we shall see face to face. Now I know in part; then I shall know fully, even as I am fully known. And now these three remain: faith, hope and love. But the greatest of these is love. — 1 Corinthians 13 (NIV)

If you look at the characteristics of love in the above chapter and realize that the love described there doesn't seem to be part of your life, you should stop right there because without love there is nothing else. I encourage you to stop and take some time to ask God to show you how you have been living. If you are really brave, you might ask someone close to you to evaluate you according to those qualities.

I want to clarify that I don't believe a person is a child of God only if he or she always walks perfectly and never sins. John says, *"No one who is born of God will continue to sin, because God's seed remains in him; he cannot go on sinning, because he has been born of God."* (1 John 3:9).

John is referring to our lifestyle. Someone who is being transformed will willfully practice holiness while a person who has stalled, gone backwards, or hasn't even begun transformation willfully practices sin. This is hard, but I would encourage you to view the list of the "fruit of the flesh" in Galatians and ask God to point out to you any of them that are in your heart. Which ones are you willfully participating in?

> The acts of the sinful nature are obvious: sexual immorality, impurity and debauchery; idolatry and witchcraft; hatred, discord, jealousy, fits of rage, selfish ambition, dissensions, factions and envy; drunkenness, orgies, and the like. I warn you, as I did before, that those who live like this will not inherit the kingdom of God. — Galatians 5:19-21 (NIV)

In this passage the Greek word Paul uses for "those who live like this" means "practice." Paul is saying that those who practice the sinful nature will not inherit the kingdom of God. There are some today who teach that we can live according to the flesh and still be welcome into the kingdom of God. Some teach that we can live in sin and still be blessed. And some teach that when we live in sin, we won't be blessed, but we will still enter the kingdom in the end as long as we have prayed the "sinner's prayer." None of this is what Jesus taught. He taught that it's those who live by the Spirit who will be welcomed into His kingdom. The Bible teaches that it's those who are being conformed to the image of Jesus who will be given seats in the heavenly places (Rom. 8:29; Eph. 2:6). Paul states clearly in the passage above that those who live a lifestyle of sin will not enter the kingdom of God. I am not teaching a "works" gospel. We don't "work" our way into the kingdom, but if we are truly born again, there will be fruit to testify to a true transformation (James. 2:20).

One night I was sitting with the Lord, and He laid a song on my heart:

I cry out to you from the depths
My soul is troubled and in pain
My sin has been raised before my eyes
And I see what your hand has revealed
Tell me oh Lord how to be clean and pure once again

Lord I need a clean heart
I need my spirit to be renewed
Please don't turn away your child for I'm crying out tonight
Return the joy I've lost and lift me up in your arms
All of my strength is gone and I need your love to rescue me
Lord renew me, Lord renew me
Is it too late, have I done too much?

Have I disqualified myself from grace?
Will you still wash me in your river?
Can you still cleanse me from the mess?
It there still mercy waiting for me?

Lord I need a clean heart
I need my spirit to be renewed
Please don't turn away your child for I'm crying out tonight
Return the joy I've lost and lift me up in your arms
All of my strength is gone and I need your love to rescue me
Lord renew me, Lord renew me

Your hand reaches out and calls me closer
I'm aware of your glory all around

Forgiveness covers me and love washes away my sin
My Daddy still loves me and is waiting for my embrace

Lord I need a clean heart
I need my spirit to be renewed
Please don't turn away your child for I'm crying out tonight
Return the joy I've lost and lift me up in your arms
All of my strength is gone and I need your love to rescue me

Lord renew me, Lord renew me

If your heart is crying out right now for transformation the way mine was the night the Lord gave me that song, then answer the call. The first step is a commitment to Jesus. Tell Him how much you need Him in your life. The next step is true repentance. The first thing John the Baptist, Peter, and even Jesus preached was repentance. That tells me it's significant. Spend some time asking Father to forgive you for every specific thing He brings to your mind. The next step is freedom from demonic strongholds and captivity. Pull down the strongholds with truth, and cast the enemy out of your life in the name of Jesus! Bind those spirits of fear, bitterness, self-hate, addictions, and others, and tell them to let go of you.

The next step is obedience. Obey Jesus, even if it means plunging into the wilderness.

The journey of transformation isn't easy. The road is narrow, and we must pick up our crosses daily (Luke 9:23). But we will never walk alone. God will always be right there with us to give us the courage and strength we need. And with each step toward the goal, we become more grounded in love and filled with all the fullness of God (Eph. 3:13-19).

Questions for Thought

- In what ways are you desperate for God? Have you been approaching God only for relief from your circumstances?
- Do you feel like you're living a lifestyle of repentance? In what areas of your life do you see a need for repentance?

- What are the strongholds in your life that are protecting the enemy's grasp on you? What events led to those strongholds? Take a moment to find the truth in Scripture that will combat the lies making up your particular stronghold.

- How have you dealt with the wilderness in your life? In what ways has the wilderness brought you closer to God? Separated you from God?

- In what ways has the past directed your present choices?

- In what ways do you feel like you have been transformed in the past?

- In what ways do you feel like you are still being transformed?

- In what ways is the "fruit" of your life bearing witness to your transformation?

CHAPTER 11

THE POWER OF GOD IS WITH YOU, PART THREE

*"That is what it means to be saved. You declare that you belong
to another system of things. People point to you and say, 'Oh,
yes, that is a Christian family; they belong to the Lord!' That
is the salvation which the Lord desires for you, that by your
public testimony you declare before God, 'My world has gone; I am
entering into another.'" – Watchman Nee*

Grocery Store Encounter

It was getting late one afternoon, and I suddenly came face to
face with a problem. We had four, five-gallon water jugs for our
water cooler, and they were all empty. So I loaded them into the
trunk and headed out to the grocery store to fill them up.

The water system was set up just inside the grocery store. I
made my way over and began the tedious process of filling the
jugs. Everything was going fine, and I was about halfway done
when a man that I instantly recognized walked by me, heading
for the exit.

An older man, he was a good friend from a church I used to
attend. It had been a few years since I had seen him. I remembered

that the desire of this man's heart had always been for the Lord. We'd had our disagreements on different things, but his love for God was completely obvious to me. He was someone I admired.

Even though I hadn't seen him for quite some time, I recognized that something was different. He looked worn out and weighed down. I called his name, and he turned. He saw me, and a tired smile spread across his face as he shook my hand and asked how I was. We made small talk for a few minutes and caught up a little. As we talked the Holy Spirit was moving in my heart and giving me insight into the current condition of my friend. I remembered him being a source of encouragement and joy, but the Lord was showing me that the joy had been stolen, allowing hopelessness and discouragement in.

I was still trying to discern what God wanted me to do when our conversation came to an end. My friend said good-bye and walked out the door. Instantly I heard voice of the Lord in my heart telling me to go pray for him, so I left my water jugs and quickly walked outside. My friend wasn't too far away, and it only took me a second to catch up to him.

He turned as I called his name, and I asked him if I could pray for him. He told me I could, and in the middle of people walking all around us, I began to pray for my friend. The Lord began to reveal the pain of my friend's heart and then began to speak words of love and encouragement. The Lord began to speak through me about how my friend's heart had lost hope, but that He was there to restore hope and build my friend up again with love. Every word was being directed straight to my friend's heart, piercing it like an arrow. All of the people around us seemed to fade, leaving just God and us.

When I finished praying, my friend lifted his head and smiled a real smile. He thanked me and shared a little of what had been happening in his life. What my friend needed was for his Father God to touch his heart, and that's what happened. We both said good-bye and walked away with our hearts full of joy.

The Ultimate Test of Obedience: Vito Rallo, retired contractor and co-founder of Free Indeed Ministries of Tampa Bay

Back in the summer of 2000, my wife and I attended what was called a "Jesus 2000 Conference" on a Thursday evening in St. Louis. It was held in the huge Edward Jones Dome. This conference was an attempt to bring all streams of different denominations together, in unity, including many Protestant denominations and Roman Catholics.

During the course of the evening, several well-known speakers had been given fifteen-minute segments of speaking time. About halfway through the evening, there was a point at which the host of the event announced that if anyone had a prophetic word from the Lord, they were invited to come forward.

I had a "word" that was burning inside. My heart was pounding so much I thought it was going to jump out of my chest, but I decided not to share the word. There were just too many nationally well-known individuals on the stage. I was intimidated by their titles and statuses. I said, "Lord, I'm not going to do it!"

Again I heard the announcer say, "Does anyone have a word from the Lord?" I knew they were speaking to me. Again I silently said no.

I soon learned that it was a big mistake not to obey when the Lord was prompting me to prophesy. He quickly reprimanded me and said, "Son, if you are not willing to give the words I give you to give to others, I'll not use you anymore. I'll find someone else." I knew in retrospect that it was a very important word from the Lord, and I was the one He had chosen to deliver it to thousands of people.

I began to shake all over, and I was so grieved at my own disobedience and His stern rebuke, that I quickly repented and said to Him, "Lord, from now on, no matter who you tell me to speak to, or wherever it might be, or whatever the circumstances, I will obey You when You want to use me in the gift of prophesy that You have given me."

With a promise like that, I was sure to be tested. And sure enough, *the ultimate test* came only a few months later.

My wife and I were driving to Atlanta to visit some family members, and we stopped somewhere in a small town in Kentucky to fill up the car with gas and to use the restrooms. When I opened the restroom door, I saw a man standing at the facility trying to—well, you know... I quickly did my business, and as I washed my hands I noticed a very worn-looking Bible on the vanity. I said a quick hello to the man and got out of there. I went back to the car and started to turn the ignition key, when I heard that still, small voice saying, "I want you to minister to him." I said, "What? That has to be the devil talking to me! You must be kidding!" The voice came again, "I want you to minister to him."

I recalled the past summer and vividly remembered the day that I refused to prophesy at the conference, when I had made the promise that I would never again refuse the Lord in that way.

I said, "Okay, Lord, but please, I beg you, don't let anyone else come in while I am ministering to this man!" I was impressed of the Lord to give the man one of my books, and so I grabbed a copy and told my wife I'd be right back. I must say that I walked back to the men's room and opened the door reluctantly. Unbelievably, the man was still standing there at the urinal, still unable to "do his business." I thought, "Great! You know, there's an unwritten code of ethics that men don't even look at one another in the restroom, much less have a conversation at the urinal!"

I timidly approached the man, keeping my distance, and said, "I have a book here that may help you get through what you are going through. I'm going to lay it here by your book." He said, "Okay, thank you." I then said, "Are you doing okay?" He said, "I'm having a real hard time with my health, and I'm holding unforgiveness toward God, asking Him why He took my beautiful wife and left me with only my son." He went on to say, "Before she died a year ago, I was a minister. I have since left the ministry because I feel that God has really let me down."

I said to him, "You know, God has a reason for everything He does. We may not understand the things that happen to us, but God does. God can heal us both physically and spiritually. I came back in here because I believe God wants me to pray for you. Would that be okay with you?" He said, "Please, I would like that."

As I began to pray for him—still keeping my distance—I heard the Lord say, "Now put your hand on his back and pray for him." So I did, and unbelievably both his hands shot up straight in the air as he began to weep profusely. At that point, I was saying to myself, "Lord, please don't let anyone come in here!" After all, this was a public, *unlocked* restroom.

My prayer quickly turned into a prophecy, a word from the Lord straight to his heart. I continued to speak the word of the Lord for several minutes as He was revealing many things about the man's life. At the same time, I was hoping and praying that no one would come in and think I was robbing this man—or something worse.

As the word came to a close, the man was shaking and sobbing like a baby. As soon as I finished prophesying, he turned around and wanted to hug me. I said, "Oh, no, that's okay." Then he wanted to shake my hand! I said, "No, that's alright, I was just being obedient to the Lord." The man told me that since his wife had passed away, he was struggling in a lot of areas, including a new prostate problem. He said that the word I gave him was just what he needed to encourage him to move past what had happened to him and that now he knew he should be obedient and go back into ministry.

He thanked me profusely, and I said, "You're welcome. Now I must be on my way." I went back out to the car and told my wife. She could not believe what had just happened, and neither could I. I will not soon forget that experience, *but a promise to the Lord is a promise,* and whenever He wants to use us, there is always a good reason. Sometimes we just have to get beyond our own "flesh" and our own "reasoning" to be used of the Lord. I believe this man was not only encouraged, but also restored and healed that day.

I may never know all that happened in that restroom to the man whose name I didn't even know. All I know is that I did my part, and I know that God did His part. Never be surprised at how the Lord may want to use you. By His grace, I have not gone back on my promise, and there have been many unusual circumstances in which I have been used, but none quite like that one!

The Nine-Minute Miracle: Patricia Rallo, co-founder of Free Indeed Ministries of Tampa Bay

One Saturday morning, several years ago, the telephone rang. I picked it up to hear a rather excited and very distraught young woman on the other end of the line. She told me that her son, who was around twelve years old (as I remember), had done something very strange at the dinner table the night before.

As the family was eating, the woman noticed that her son had cut marks on both arms. She asked him, "What happened to you? How did those marks get there?" He put his head down for a few seconds, and when he raised his head up to look at her, his whole countenance suddenly changed. It no longer looked like her son, and there was a very evil, dark look in his eyes. Something had taken over her son! He just stared blankly at her and never did answer her question.

After dinner the woman went into her son's room and began questioning him again. He began to become completely out of control—screaming and becoming violent and flailing. She began to scream in fear, and her husband quickly ran to see what was going on. They somehow got the boy in the car and took him to the hospital. The doctors and nurses tried and tried to diagnose the problem. After many questions, a few tests, and much probing, they never did discover the cause of the problem, so they released him, and the three of them went back home.

This Christian woman had been praying that Saturday morning, asking the Lord to show her the root cause of her son's problem. As she relayed the story to me, I began to ask her several pertinent questions. I learned that the woman's husband had recently introduced their son to the game Dungeons & Dragons, and they had been playing it together for quite a while. This type of game and similar ones will always give the enemy of our soul access into our lives, and unfortunately this same scenario is played out in many families. It is not innocent fun, as many believe. As the woman had been praying that morning, the Holy Spirit had revealed to her that the game was the reason that a demonic presence had been invited into her son's life. It had been given access—a legal right to be there.

The woman had already talked that morning to her husband, for whose salvation she had been praying for nine years, although he had not yet accepted Jesus into his life. He had adamantly stated that there was no way he was going to give up the game. So she had called me while her husband had taken their son out to run some errands that morning.

We talked for about a half an hour or so, and I discerned that she was spiritually mature and astute. I told her that, as a believer, she had authority over evil spirits, but only if they were willing to get rid of the game, to get it out of their house completely, because it had brought in all kinds of demonic spirits, such as the one that had influenced the son to begin cutting himself. I taught her how to bind and break the power of all evil that had invaded her home, and I assured her that it was "in Jesus' name" that we (as believers) have power over evil, tormenting spirits. We ended our conversation, and I continued to pray about this situation.

About an hour later, I got another phone call from the woman. This time she was also very excited—but no longer distraught. She told me that her son and her husband had come back from the store, and she had tried to reason with her husband once again, in the hopes that he would understand the spiritual ramifications of what would happen if he did not agree to get rid of Dungeons & Dragons.

Her husband began to argue with her once again, and the son came running out of his room and exclaimed, "Why are you fighting?" The son began to manifest again. His voice changed, his

143

face changed, and everything was like it had been the night before. Only this time, the woman knew what to do. She immediately took authority over the evil spirit and declared: "In the name of Jesus, I bind the spirit that is tormenting my son, and I break your power! I command you to leave right now, and never again to return!"

The son was miraculously and immediately delivered! The husband was shocked and speechless, utterly amazed at how quickly his son became calm and peaceful. Because the husband had just witnessed, for the first time, the delivering power of the Lord Jesus Christ, it caused him to repent and give his heart to the Lord on the spot! Immediately he agreed to get rid of Dungeons & Dragons and anything else that might be a spiritual hindrance in their home. The son was in full agreement.

Seeing all this, the boy turned, and in his right mind excitedly said to his mother, "Look, Mom, God did in nine minutes what you couldn't do in nine years!" Thank God He is still healing, delivering, and performing miracles today.

I was led by the Holy Spirit that day to take the time to encourage and equip this woman to use *her authority*, rather than having her be dependent on me. Ordinarily I would have had them come as a family for my husband and myself to counsel, but that day was different. God can move any way He wants and chooses, as long as we are willing to be flexible and to yield to His leading. I was reminded again that day that it is important that we do not try to confine God to a *pre-determined method* or to the same *formula* each time we have the opportunity to minister to someone.

CHAPTER 12

OBEDIENCE

"Our Lord told His disciples that love and obedience were organically united. The final test of love is obedience." – A.W. Tozer

More and more I am coming to understand that almost every time God calls me to an act of obedience, I don't want to do it. Whether it is out of frustration, discomfort, or rebellion, my first reaction is almost always hesitance.

Obedience is a choice. We have to engage our will to do the things God asks us to do. I guess that's why the rewards of obedience are so great and the consequences of disobedience are so severe. In every choice we make, we tell God whom we love the most.

I have taken many sick people to the hospital over the years. After beginning the journey of transformation, I have allowed God to move through me in the midst of my job, and I have seen some amazing things. I have seen hope restored with a prayer and freedom gained through a prophetic word. I have ministered deliverance in the back of the rescue and seen captives set free from demons. I have seen miraculous healings, and I have seen God raise the dead. You would think that seeing all of these things would make me want to obey without any hesitation.

I learned a lot about obedience when I was struggling with compassion. Sometimes holding onto compassion is a very difficult thing, especially in doing what I do for a living. We transport many people to the hospital who called 911 because they felt "tingly" in their fingers or because their toes hurt or because they had a dry mouth. It can be very easy for compassion to fade. Before I know it, I can easily begin judging people and become angry. But Jesus' ministry was full of compassion. God is love. Compassion is rooted in love, and so if we lose compassion, we really lose sight of God.

I remember a specific time when my compassion had been under attack, and a degree of hardness had ebbed its way into my heart. We were called to a woman who was complaining of a headache that had been going on for three days. She said it had become worse, and she wanted us to take her to the hospital. It was not a migraine. It was just a nuisance to her. It was certainly not an emergency in my opinion, and I was annoyed. The woman took forever to get out of the house. It seemed like she had fifty things she wanted to do before she left, and I was doing everything short of actually pulling her out of the door. I judged her as just another person abusing the system. My compassion for her was zero. Finally, we loaded her up and started toward the hospital. I was interacting with the woman as little as I could. She talked to me about her life, and I was trying really hard not to listen.

When we were a few minutes from the hospital, she did something I wasn't prepared for, and it made me mad. She asked me to pray for her. I did not want to pray for this woman. I was thinking, *"Really? You call me for a headache, abuse 911, take forever to get out of the house, and you want me to pray for you?"* I knew God wanted me to pray for her, but I decided in my heart that I wouldn't. I told her I would pray for her, but I didn't.

We pulled into the hospital a minute later and took her into the ER. The whole way in I was under constant, heavy conviction for being disobedient. We put her in the bed assigned to her, and I couldn't take the conviction any longer. I looked at her and said, "Did you want me to pray for you?" She said yes, and I said a quick, mildly annoyed prayer without much feeling at all.

146

When I was done, I looked at her. Her eyes were tearing up as she began to open up to me about many very painful and terrible things she had been through. It was like a floodgate opened. The woman whom I hadn't really treated very well poured out her heart to me. To tell the truth, I was actually annoyed at the development. God had used me to minister to many people, and I knew that's where it was heading, but I was still mad at her. I still had to make a choice in that moment to be obedient.

As the woman continued to share, God melted the hardness in my heart, and I decided to forgive the woman and allow God to work through me. As I said yes to God, I felt compassion and love come back in full force. My annoyance and anger left, and I proceeded to minister to the woman prophetically. As I spoke the words God gave me to speak, I could see the work going on in the woman's spirit and soul. There was a battle taking place. God planted a seed with a call to action in her. She was deeply touched and emotional. I was filled with joy; what a privilege to be used by God in that way!

I don't know what happened to that woman. I hope to see her in the kingdom some day. But I learned some lessons. God can definitely use us in spite of ourselves. A half-sincere prayer is what God used to open the gates for that woman. I learned, once again, the joys of obedience. I became painfully aware of lost compassion, which led me to some deep repentance and the restoration of my relationship with God. I learned, once again, that obedience is always a choice. Every call to obedience is significant, and you can almost guarantee that your initial reaction is going to be "I don't want to" every time. The question God is asking is, "Whom do you love the most?"

I have come to understand that our transformation is only as good as our willingness to be obedient.

"If ye be willing and obedient, ye shall eat the good of the land." — Isaiah 1:19

We may know the right words to say to give people the impression that we are living a godly life, but if obedience isn't a part of our walk, I don't think we are eating the "good of the land". I lived a long time just saying the things I knew I should say, but I was living a disobedient and rebellious lifestyle. I walked in bitterness, self-hatred and fear. I sinned with pornography, lust, and gambling. I was selfish, and in most decisions I considered how I would be affected first. I was a far cry from eating the "good of the land". I was eating garbage. Only when I began to choose obedience did I experience God's abundant blessings as He did amazing things in my life.

Have you ever been obedient and ended up disappointed with the results of your obedience? Has obedience ever brought you pain? Three days after responding to the woman who had drowned, about whom I shared earlier, I was able to check on her at the hospital. What I found out was that the husband was getting ready to disconnect life support. They had found a large brain bleed. When I heard this, I was upset and disappointed. That wasn't the way it was supposed to end. She was supposed to leave the hospital alive and well. Did the outcome take away from the miracle? It felt like it did. What was the point? Why give her three more days? It seemed like a cruel joke. I thought, *"I put myself out there by telling people about this miracle, and now look. God is supposed to raise people from the dead and then keep them alive!"* I felt cheated. I felt like God gave me a front seat to see Him move in power, and then a couple of days later took away a huge chunk of that experience. I felt deflated. I wondered why I should even bother being obedient.

I spent most of the next day processing everything I was feeling. Here is what I believe God revealed: our idea of a proper outcome and what God actually does many times don't match. I was disappointed when the miracle didn't look the way I thought it should look, and I even began to question the miracle. Where did my understanding a resurrection miracle come from? Why did I feel like I could predict an unpredictable God? God really hammered me with the truth that nothing has to look the way what I say it should. But something in me still wanted to say that it does. A resurrection miracle has to be when the person is fully restored to the quality of life they once had. Why? Because I say so?

There are many things I don't know about why this happened. But here are some that I do know. I saw a dead woman come back to life. Because of the three extra days, her family had a chance to come together and say good-bye. Her husband had the opportunity to let her go on his terms. God gave him the chance to give her away instead of her being snatched away from him. I have no idea how God worked in the hearts of these people over that three extra days but I know that there was great purpose in them. And let's consider the fact that the people whom Jesus raised from the dead in the Bible still passed away later on. I'm pretty sure Lazarus isn't still walking today. If he is, I'd really like to meet him. We don't know how long Lazarus lived after Jesus called him out of the tomb. Was it three days, three months, or thirty years? We don't know. But does the fact that Lazarus eventually died take away from the miracle of Jesus raising him from the dead? What difference does it make if it was three days or thirty years? Does time qualify the miracle?

There is so much I don't understand about God, but I am starting to understand that the miracles and testimonies are not just about the miracle itself. They are also about how God moves in the lives and hearts of everyone involved, and even beyond. It's never just about us or the person receiving the miracle. In the miracles in the Bible, there always seems to be something so much deeper and far-reaching than the event itself.

God allows me to be a part of miracles for reasons I see, but also for many reasons that I don't see. What I know from my experience with the woman who drowned is this: God only needed three days to do what He wanted to through the miracle. And through the experience, He really showed me some ungodly beliefs and expectations that were residing in my heart.

Obedience doesn't always bring about a pleasurable result externally. If you have ever tried to be "set apart" in an environment where people don't love Jesus, you know what I mean. Obedience will often cause division and conflict because when we walk in obedience to God, we are taking the true gospel wherever we go. The true gospel of Jesus is offensive to those who are walking in disobedience (1 Pet. 2:8). However, obedience will always bring about a pleasurable experience on the inside. Every act of obedience moves us closer to God and further from the clutches of the enemy. Here are some passages about obedience:

> For as by one man's disobedience many were made sinners, so by the obedience of one shall many be made righteous. — Romans 5:19

Paul is talking about Adam and Jesus in this passage. I find this passage extremely important when we realize that it was the obedience of Jesus that provided salvation to all who come to Him. I find it even more significant when we realize that obedience was something that Jesus himself had to learn through suffering.

> Though he were a Son, yet learned he obedience by the things which he suffered. — Hebrews 5:8

Obedience to God will come with a cost. Obedience can cost us much of what we have grown comfortable with. Jesus is not apologetic about this, and He tells us to count the cost (Luke 14:28). We have the world to lose, but we have the kingdom of God to gain.

> Don't you know that when you offer yourselves to someone as obedient slaves, you are slaves of the one you obey—whether you are slaves to sin, which leads to death, or to obedience, which leads to righteousness? — Romans 6:16 (NIV)

Obedience brings righteousness.

> Another reason I wrote you was to see if you would stand the test and be obedient in everything. — 2 Corinthians 2:9 (NIV)

Obedience proves our character.

> Jesus replied, "If anyone loves me, he will obey my teaching. My Father will love him, and we will come to him and make our home with him. He who does not love me will not obey my teaching. These words you hear are not my own; they belong to the Father who sent me." — John 14:23-24 (NIV)

Our obedience is the testimony of our love for Jesus. Our disobedience and rebellion is the testimony of our love for ourselves.

It's not easy to be obedient. The choice is ours to make, and the enemy always shows us that disobedience is an easier road. The wide path is easy. The narrow path is hard. It takes great courage to be obedient, and it takes our will to make the hard choices. The strength to trust and not fear, to forgive and not harbor bitterness, and to choose God instead of every worldly pleasure is available, but we have to make the choice to obey. Nobody is going to make that choice for us.

I have seen many people who have been set free from the enemy allow captivity back into their lives because, when it came time to make the hard choice, they chose the old way. We will be attacked by the enemy in the areas where we have experienced freedom. He will bring everything he can against us in order to regain lost ground. He will bring family and friends against us. He will position people around us who will tempt us to go back to the old way. He will try to steal all of our money and all of our possessions. Other times he might increase money in an effort to distract or entice greed and self-sufficiency. He is ruthless and will do anything he can to try and make obedience seem impossible.

But obedience is choosing to react differently to all of those different stressors. When something comes to make you anxious, react with faith. When something makes you angry, react with forgiveness. When the temptation of addiction comes, react with the knowledge that the perfect love of God has saturated your heart, and you don't need anything else to make you feel loved.

When your money is gone and possessions lost, react with trust in the promises of Matthew 6. Jesus promises that if we choose obedience we will have everything that we need every single day! Not everything that we want, but everything that we need. Kara and I have walked through times when we had forty dollars or less to our name. We are a family of four. We chose to trust in God's promise instead of making choices motivated by fear, and every single day we had food, shelter, and clothing. Every bill was paid, and the cars never ran out of gas. We learned and grew so much during those times.

Obedience is the most effective form of deliverance there is. We get freedom by repenting and casting the enemy out of our life. We stay free by walking in obedience in the face of the enemy's onslaught. Nothing will make the enemy flee faster than obedience. Keep him on the run!

> Submit yourselves therefore to God. Resist the devil, and he will flee from you. — James 4:7

Questions for Thought

- In what ways is it a struggle for you to be obedient to God?
- How has obedience brought joy to your life? How has it been painful to be obedient?
- In what areas of your life do you need to make the choice to be obedient to God?

CHAPTER 13

THE BRIDE

And I saw a new heaven and a new earth: for the first heaven and the first earth were passed away; and there was no more sea. And I John saw the holy city, new Jerusalem, coming down from God out of heaven, prepared as a bride adorned for her husband. And I heard a great voice out of heaven saying, Behold, the tabernacle of God is with men, and he will dwell with them, and they shall be his people, and God himself shall be with them, and be their God. And God shall wipe away all tears from their eyes; and there shall be no more death, neither sorrow, nor crying, neither shall there be any more pain: for the former things are passed away.
— Revelation 21:1-4

As I think about Jesus and what He wants His relationship with us to be like, I get a little sad. Not because of anything related to Jesus. I get sad because our response to His call, on a large scale, is tragic. Jesus calls us His Bride, but many of us don't understand that call or are unwilling to conform to that awesome image. Our ignorance and rebellion cause us to trample on the love He is extending. We are chased and pursued by the love of God, yet many of us live our whole lives wishing that someone would truly love us, convinced that nobody cares. Why isn't the church running into the arms of its greatest and most passionate lover, Jesus? Why are we walking around in "rags" when Jesus is trying to direct us toward the changing room, holding beautiful wedding garments?

If we could only see the filth of the rags we hold so close and smell the stink, we would exchange them in an instant. But many of us don't. We have been blinded to it, and our noses have been numbed to the stench. We have even called the filth beautiful and the stench a sweet fragrance. The things we have obtained and everything we have accomplished are exalted before us, and we see them as glamorous, unaware that our souls are rotting. The fear, bitterness, and insecurities we hold so tightly are comfortable to us. We have formed our identities in the world instead of realizing that God has already laid the groundwork for our identities to be in Him.

We hold onto our rags as we go to church every week and meet in small groups. We talk and listen, but our rags have formed a barrier in our hearts, and we don't receive conviction. We brush it off, determining in our hearts that we don't need to change. We just shrug and say, "God knows my heart," even though the fruit of our hearts shows we don't love God at all. We trample all over the sacrifice Jesus made.

The following is a word from the Lord received by a man named Phil Buck. It really made an impact on me and so I want to include it here.

Earthquake in the Church—A Word

January 27, 2010—Prayer time for the Church at our home.

I heard a word in my mind saying, "There's coming an earthquake of the magnitude 7.0 that was experienced in Haiti, only it is coming to the Church. I have sent many warnings down through the portals of time that this day was coming, and now it is here, even at the door. The earthquake will start from outside the Church, and then will permeate the Church from within. Prepare, prepare, there will be destruction as would never have been imagined.

"The rubble of the buildings of man will crumble to the ground. The teachings of man will have come full circle. There will be people that have bought into the man system and will be destroyed in the rubble of the collapse, some spiritually and others both spiritually and physically. For they have believed a lie and will suffer the consequences of their doing."

"Of those that have escaped, I see a long line extending beyond my vision to see. They are the walking wounded from all religious persuasions that were not caught up totally in the man-centered religious system of beliefs. But being exposed to the system has left its mark in various forms on each one.

"I see this line in my mind's eye, people lined up at the entrance to a white tent. This is where they are coming to receive life, spiritual life from inside the tent. Those inside the tent are like doctors and nurses, ministering to the wounded, hurting spirits of each one. As they help them heal, with the proper perspective and focus of the gifts they have to offer, then they are sent from the tent whole and ready to minister to others as they were ministered to.

"Now behold the ones on the inside of the tent, before they stepped inside the tent they had nothing to offer in and of themselves, but as they stepped in they received the power to work the works for which I have called them to. This is a special people who have closed themselves up with me. Yes, and some have been in preparation all their lives for this time and this mission.

"I want you to see those in the tent, for they are those that have given everything to Me. These are they that this day I'm calling to come out of the religious systems of man and into the marvelous light of my Son Jesus. Will you be counted as numbered among those in the tent? Or will you be one of the many in the long line?

"Come away with Me this day and give your all to Me for the line is long and is now just beginning to form. They need your gifts, your love, and your sacrifice of service. Will you be there for them? Or will you be among them?"

Jesus is coming for a pure and spotless Bride. He is coming for those who have forsaken the world and aligned themselves to Him. He is coming for those who have become aware of the stinking rags and have exchanged them for garments of praise.

There is an awakening happening across the land. God is waking up his remnant. There are many people across America and across the world who are being shaken out of their complacency and becoming alive in Christ. Those people are truly searching for truth and finding a real relationship with their Daddy (God). The blindness is being stripped away from those desperate people as they cry out in repentance and for freedom in every area of their lives.

Those people are turning their backs on the traditions of man, however uncomfortable it makes them and others feel, and are rising up with revelation of the true message of the gospel. The refining period those people have walked through has led to much discomfort and pain in their lives as they allow God to pull out the weeds buried in their souls. But as they are purged, new seeds of life are planted. They are becoming new creations as the "old man" dies. They are reacting with love and experiencing a change in their character that they really can't explain. They are being transformed and are stepping into their identity as the beloved children of God and the Bride of Jesus.

The awakening is happening in the traditional churches as a few members are becoming desperate for more. Unfortunately, the desperation many times collides with the church leadership in conflict as the few push for change and the many resist. The awakening is also happening outside of the traditional church as people are becoming alive in Christ and meeting together in homes. We are part of home gatherings and are seeing God do amazing things. I think it's important, though, to keep in mind that none of us can claim spiritual supremacy, regardless of the type of church we are in community with.

I found a great article from Andrew Strom that speaks to this issue.

In-Church, Out-of-Church, Future Church

by Andrew Strom

I have met and fellowshipped with many wonderful Christian people over the years from all kinds of backgrounds. But I just

156

need to comment on this "in-church/out-of-church" thing because it keeps cropping up.

Let me be clear about this. I meet wonderful "in-church" people all the time that I absolutely love. And I meet lovely "out-of-church" people, too, that I absolutely love. One of the biggest problems is that often these two groups do not understand each other at all. And neither do they necessarily see the need for a "future church" that is beyond anything that any of us are seeing—a church that is literally just like the Book of Acts. That is supposed to be our goal. But too often we are satisfied basically where we are.

Challenges for the In-Church

Many of the Christians who are totally in the church system truly see the need for change. They do not want to sit still. They see there has been a great decline in Christianity away from the old paths. And they are praying that God will move to restore and purify His Bride. I have met many godly, warm-hearted people like this who care passionately about God's kingdom and His true gospel. I usually get on very well with such ones because we share a common desire to see things righted, especially the gospel message that has become so diluted and lost.

I guess the biggest challenge that I see in these settings is that I believe God is about to move outside the box in such a drastic way that if we allow ourselves to be too attached to the current system or way of church, then we can easily get left behind. To get us back to true Book of Acts Christianity will take such a leap and such change that I wonder if we truly have it in us to go with Him where He wants to go. How loosely do we hold all these things—our buildings, our meeting formats, our labels, titles, and ways of doing things? When these things are shaken or challenged, it is sometimes surprising to discover what a hold they have on us, even if we think they don't. This is the biggest challenge that the system-type people face, I believe. But our love of the true gospel and true Bible Christianity will take us a long way.

Challenges for the Out-of-Church

I have moved amongst many house-church- and out-of-church-type Christians (which are not the same thing) over the years. In fact I have been part of these circles myself at times. One of the biggest problems I have seen is that some of us really thought we had the major answer to the church's problems. Those of us in the 'house-church' movement would think, "If only the church would get out of buildings and into houses and become more relational, most of our problems would be solved!" We truly thought that simply by changing boxes, we could get back the Book of Acts church! What we ended up with, of course, were simply the same people in a different shell—slightly more relational, but hardly anything like the power and purity of the early Christians. We had changed the outward form, but the power of Jesus Christ was still mostly lacking.

I can remember having arguments over plurality of eldership, the precise correct way of taking the Lord's Supper, and all kinds of things. None of it seemed to make the slightest bit of difference. That is because the outward things and the form of things are all secondary. This is not where the power is. But it took such a long time to learn this lesson.

The out-of-church people are even more radical. They often fellowship with almost no one, and many of them will tell you that the organized church is the "whore of Babylon," etc. A lot of them are lovely people with a real heart for people and for truth. But some can be very judgmental and harsh. They will often write off church people as being totally bound by religion. But I found many of us in that circle had our own anti-religion religion going on! We despised having leaders or organized things of any kind. We said we believed in the five-fold ministries, but we couldn't stand to have any actual leaders, even godly ones. And we were secretly filled with pride because we could see everything that was wrong with the system. Man, did I have a humbling coming when I got into this mindset! I was so religiously anti-religious. I was so filled with arrogance and looked down my nose at so many system people! I judged them just because they went to a building on Sunday! God forgive me.

Of course, none of this is the answer either. I had to repent. I had to renounce very deeply this harsh anti-religion religion that made me so proud and arrogant towards people. I found that many of them loved Jesus just as much as I did. And many of them prayed more and were kinder, more loving, and godlier than I'd ever been. I had been kidding myself. When it boiled right down, we out-of-church types were no closer to the Book of Acts than many of the system people that we judged so harshly. We just knew more stuff (supposedly). But clearly it wasn't the stuff that mattered.

It was only when I deeply repented and renounced this whole prideful mindset that God gradually began to show me what was really important. And it was not the outward stuff, though of course there is some importance to structure, etc.

I believe each of these things (below) will be a crucial part of the Future Church that God wants to bring about. You could literally write a book about each one, they are so important. It was these very things that meant that the early church showed forth the glory of Jesus every day. Here they are.

We must have:

1. An **Apostolic gospel** being preached with Apostolic-type anointing and authority. (Whenever this has happened down through history, there has been real revival). So crucial.

2. The powerful moving of the **Holy Spirit** filling people, healing people, convicting people, transforming people.

3. **Real love** and an emphasis on ministering to the **poor**. (Just like the early church.)

4. **Real disciples** who actually forsake all to follow Jesus.

5. **Real prayer** in the Holy Spirit. And lots of it!!

6. **The whole body ministering**, starting with the five-fold ministries, whose goal is to release the whole body into ministry.

7. **Miracles and healings**. These are a must!

Of course, we could go on and on. But let me just conclude by saying this. It doesn't matter if we are in-church, out-of-church, over-churched, or under-churched. If we don't have the above things, which the early church had in abundance, then we really don't have anything. It doesn't matter what we know or whether we meet in houses, barns, on the streets or in sun-porches. If we don't have these crucial things that the early church majored on, then we really have nothing that matters.

So I don't really care if you are out-churched, over-churched, thru-churched, or half-churched. We need to pursue and pursue until we get real Christianity back! None of us have got it, so we had all better repent of our pride and start seeking that which is lost! A glorious Bride beckons. What price are we willing to pay to see her glory restored?

That is a great word that should impact us to our core. The journey of transformation takes us into real relationship with God, secures us in love, and changes us into the Bride. We don't become the Bride just by saying we are. We become the Bride by denying our flesh and taking up our cross (Luke 9:23). We become the Bride by working out our salvation daily with fear and trembling (Phil. 2:12-13). We become the Bride by putting down pride and taking up desperation.

One night I was alone in the fire station bay seeking the Lord. I felt my spirit stirred to walk over to a kitten that a friend of mine had rescued and intended to take it home as a pet. As I walked over, the Lord began to speak to my spirit.

My church is not unlike this small kitten. You can hear the cries of sadness from a distance. (I could hear the kitten crying.) You can hear it cry out for safety and security. You can hear it cry out for protection and provision. But as you get closer and come upon it, it immediately moves to the corner shaking and hissing. (This is exactly what happened as I moved closer to the kitten.) You discover that it is nothing but a small, insecure animal that is wrapped in fear and lashes out when threatened. You discover that this little animal does not trust you and doesn't really even know you. Though all you want to do is to help and comfort it, it will not receive you, and as you stretch out your hand, it strikes at you. I come to my church, but it does not know Me. I reach out my hand, and it strikes. Fear and insecurity reign in My people. I send My prophets with My word, and they are disregarded. They are persecuted. They are turned away.

In response to my wondering what I could do or how the dynamic could change, the Lord said,

> Now consider what happens as the kitten begins to know its master. What happens as the kitten begins to trust and rely on the master? The kitten receives the master's love and even shows the master love. So will my people submit to Me as they begin to understand My love. I will bring revelations of My love to their hearts. I will begin to prick their souls. They will begin to ask and seek.

As I was considering this, I wondered what my part might be in this, and the Lord said, "Show them who I am. Help them understand My love by living in it. Bear My testimony to the people."

I want to share with you another word I received from the Lord as I was worshiping and praising Him at home. The Lord began to speak to my heart:

> "Behold! I am coming for My pure and spotless bride. Raise your head for you are the object of My love. Your Lover comes adorned in wedding garments prepared for His bride. Come and meet me in righteousness and splendor, and I will lift you high in My love. Come, for your salvation is near. Your hearts beat with love for Me, and I am coming to collect you into My arms.

> "Rest in peace and knowledge that I will never neglect, turn away from, or depart from the object of My love. Have peace, My beautiful bride, and cast away the rags that have become a part of your soul. Put on the wedding garments I have prepared for you, and join Me at the feast. For your Lover has come to cast off your burdens and to make you light—to give you hope and a future.

> "I will never leave you. I will never betray you. For My foundation is built on righteousness and holiness. I am the Lord, and you are the object of My love. Come and rest. Come and let Me rescue you from the quicksand that wants to pull you under. Take My hand, and let Me lead you. Gaze into My eyes, and understand just how much you mean to Me. Look

at My face, and look at a love far beyond anything you can understand. It's a love so overwhelming that it will take you to your knees.

"I reach for My bride. Reach back! Run to Me, and you shall experience peace. Come and draw your water from the wells of salvation with joy! Let the remnant shout, 'Look! Our Lover comes adorned in glory and splendor to deliver us and take us home!' Walk with Me in the valleys of peace, and you shall find rest for your soul."

There is a call for the remnant echoing in each soul on the earth. Those who have "ears to hear" will respond. Those with "eyes to see" will see God at work in their lives (Matt. 13:13-14). When we make the choice to respond, God builds testimonies. Before long there will be a great army on the earth defeating the enemy *"by the blood of the Lamb, and the word of their testimony"* (Rev. 12:11). Will you be a soldier in that army? I encourage you to proclaim the works of God as He leads you. Do not be ashamed of Him in whatever He has done or is doing in your life. Proclaim the works of God to your children. Shout the works of God, and the enemy's strongholds will shake and come crashing down. Walk the journey of transformation with great courage, and you too will find your Life Resurrected!

Questions for Thought

- In what ways do you feel like you are included when Christ talks about His "Bride"?

- In what ways do you feel like you aren't a part of Jesus' Bride?

- What have your experiences been with the "in-church" and the "out-of-church?

- What areas of your life do you need to commit to God in order to become "spotless" and "pure?

BIBLIOGRAPHY

Mull, R. (2008). *Lord Heal Me.* Lake Mary: Creation House

Rah, S. (2009). *The Next Evangelicalism, Releasing the Church from Western Cultural Captivity.* Downers Grove: InterVarsity Press

Frangipane, F. (1989). *The Three Battlegrounds.* Cedar Rapids: Arrow Publications

Boyd, G. (2005). *The Myth of a Christian Nation, How The Quest for Political Power is Destroying The Church.* Grand Rapids: Zondervan

Strom, A. (2010). *Earthquake in the Church.* From: http://www.johnthebaptisttv.com/forum-2/

Strom, A. *In-Church, Out-of-Church, and Future-Church.* From: http://www.johnthebaptisttv.com/forum-2/

Lehrman, B. *What Must I Do to be Saved?* From: http://www.lehrmangroup.com/verse/saved.html

Bradshaw, A. (2001) *Christian Quotes.* From: http://www.christianquotes.org/

(1999) *Christian Quotes.* From: http://christian-quotes.ochristian.com/

OTHER BOOKS *from* OPERATION LIGHT FORCE

Marriage: What's the Point Author Jesse Birkey will take you on a journey of personal tragedy as marital infidelity brought his whole world down around him. As Jesse lay in the ruins of everything he knew, he began asking questions desperate for answers. As the smoke began to clear Jesse began to hear the small, still voice of the Holy Spirit telling him that his hope for a restored marriage, and a resurrected life, rested in his willingness to be transformed. It was then that Jesus picked Jesse up and set him on the path to freedom and life and they began walking hand in hand. Take the journey in *Marriage: What's The Point?*

God Speaks: Learn How to Hear God, **by Richard Mull** In the Acts God spoke 22 different ways. Through highlighted text and commentary, you will be amazed to see how much God is speaking to His people

Justice Revolution, **by Barry Sullivan** This book will walk teens and young adults through 21 EXTREME DAYS that will open their eyes to the 7 injustices in the world and ask them to take action DAILY.

The Jesus Training Manual, **by Richard Mull** This is a life-altering book written by Richard Mull. Based solidly upon the Word of God and filled with powerful stories, Richard shares the lessons that Jesus took him through. These are some of the lessons that He taught His disciples 2,000 years ago.

Visit *OperationLightForce.com* to purchase these and other resources.

DEAR READER,

This book really impacted my life and I am sure that it impacted yours as well. You know that this book, *Life Resurrected,* will change lives. For most people, the only way they will learn of this book is from someone like you whose life was impacted by it. For others to have their lives changed, you need to put a copy of this book into their hands.

But others (seeds) fell into good ground, and brought forth fruit, some a hundred-fold, some sixty-fold, some thirty-fold (Matt. 13:8).

Our calling is to constantly seek new means of finding good ground to plant this message into. Will you help us reach other people with the life-changing message?

I have a little garden on my back porch. The more seeds that I plant, the more plants I have and the more fruit it bears. Remember that if you want a large crop you have to plant more seeds.

Consider impacting others by giving away this life-transforming book to five, ten or twenty or more people. DON'T WAIT!

Thank you,

Richard Mull

Founder Light Force Publishing and Operation Light Force

OperationLightForce

CONTACT INFORMATION

Find more information and connect with Jesse and Kara through their website *www.reflectministry.com*

Reach them through email at *jbirkey@reflectministry.com*

View and follow their blog at *jessebirkey.wordpress.com*

Follow them on Twitter at *twitter.com/JesseBirkey*

Follow them on Facebook at *http://www.facebook.com/ LifeResurrected*